BACK TO THE PRESENT

Encountering **GENESIS** in the **21**st century

by Dr Laurence Turner

Abbreviations

KJV   King James Version
NASB New American Standard Bible
NIV   New International Version
NJB   New Jerusalem Bible
NKJV New King James Version
NRSV New Revised Standard Version

First Published in 2004
Copyright © 2004
All rights reserved. No part of this publication
may be reproduced in any form without prior
permission from the publisher. British Library
Cataloguing in Publication Data.
A catalogue record for this book is
available from the British Library.

ISBN 1 903921 27 9

Design by
Abigail Murphy

Published by
Autumn House, Grantham, England

Printed in
Thailand

Encountering **GENESIS** in the **21**st century

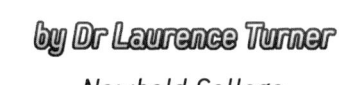

by Dr Laurence Turner

Newbold College

ABOUT THE AUTHOR

Dr Laurence Turner holds an Mdiv from Andrews University, a ThM from Princeton Theological Seminary, and a PhD from Sheffield University. He has worked as a pastor in the South of England and a lecturer at Avondale College in New South Wales. Currently he teaches at Newbold College.

Laurence is married to Anne. They have a son, Jonathan, and a daughter, Lisa. His hobbies include hiking, cooking and supporting Middlesbrough football club 'in the forlorn hope that one day they will actually win something (though we did win the amateur FA Cup back in the 1880s!)'.

'In recent years,' writes Dr Turner, 'I have spent a great deal of time studying the Bible, and also teaching and preaching it. In doing so, I've learned to appreciate everything God has given us in the Bible, but especially its stories, such as the ones we encounter in Genesis. They've never lost their power. Put simply,' he concludes, 'When I read them I hear God speaking to me.'

contents

UPFRONT

We often deal with God as if he were an object for debate, defined by creeds or circumscribed by 'fundamental beliefs'.

But in the Genesis account, God is a character, a personality, not a theological construct. . . .

He is a God we can relate to.

Genesis invites us to know and experience him. After all, we were created in his image. At the very least this means that we were created with a capacity to have a relationship with him.

If that is how God created us, clearly he wants to have a relationship with us. That would not be possible if he were the intellectual God of philosophy, or the impassive God of the ancient Greeks.

But he isn't.

He is a personal God with emotions, who grieves over our sin and suffers with us. . . .

God understands feeling and suffering.

God does judge, but that is never his first port of call.

In the pages of BACK to the PRESENT: Encountering Genesis in the 21st Century, learn to relate to a God who is eager to relate to you.

Laurence Turner
Newbold College
1 January 2004

INTRODUCTION
to the BOOK OF Genesis

We all know Genesis, even if we've never read it.

Despite our secular age, its images are still familiar: the serpent tempting Eve, the animals going into Noah's ark, Joseph in his multi-coloured coat, and so on.

Yet, at the same time, we often dismiss those images as having nothing to say to modern people. Appropriate for children, perhaps, along with nursery rhymes and fairy tales. But adults such as ourselves no longer take seriously such simple and crude narratives, created for simple and unsophisticated readers.

Which all goes to show just how wrong we are. We usually treat short stories as entertainment, a relaxing read on the beach during our annual holiday, or filling in time at the dentist. In Israel, however, stories had a much higher status. They were used to explore the great issues and problems of human existence.

If we were asked, 'What is the meaning of life?', our response, once we had reflected on the matter, would likely be a logically argued position. We would provide, to a greater or lesser extent, a 'philosophical' answer. But if you had asked an ancient Israelite the same question, the reply would have been, 'Let me tell you a story'.

That is what we discover in Genesis – stories that plumb the depths of human fear, tragedy, love, faith, hatred – the whole gamut of human experience.

Don't be fooled by their simplicity. The stories themselves are simple enough to be remembered after one reading, but they repay a lifetime of reflection because they are among the best

and most controversial ever written. That means they are as
powerful now as when first composed thousands of years ago.

This present volume will not try to tackle scientific questions
that arise from the text.[1] For one thing, science as we know it
hadn't been invented when Genesis was written. Rather, we will
explore together the spiritual resources in Genesis, investigating
what it reveals about God, ourselves and the world in which we
live. In particular, this book aims to guide you on your own journey of discovery into Genesis 1-11. We will look at the whole
section, though more emphasis will be placed on chapters 1-4
because they form the foundation for what follows. However,
reading this book is no substitute for reading Genesis itself. You
will gain far more if you read a passage from Genesis before
turning to the appropriate comments here. That way, your
engagement with Scripture will be much more rewarding.

I will apply some aspects of the biblical text, as we encounter
them, to our lives. However, before we can apply the text in any
depth we must first understand it. For that reason, the final
chapter will reflect on the whole journey undertaken, and draw
together what those chapters have revealed about God,
ourselves and the world.

Genesis has been put together with a great deal of thought.
It has two main sections. The first, stretching from Genesis 1:1-
11:26, and known as the primaeval history, starts with the creation of 'the heavens and the earth'. It then pictures human
beings disobeying God, the first murder, degeneration into
moral anarchy, the great flood that destroyed the earth, its
repopulation and, finally, the story of rebellion at Babel.

The second main section of Genesis, the ancestral history,
tells the great saga of the ancestors of ancient Israel. It begins
with God choosing old Abram to be the father of a great nation
and climaxes, against all the odds, with Sarah his wife bearing
Isaac at an age that confounded their doubts. Isaac's children
Jacob and Esau are centre-stage in the next episode, where
God's purposes are worked out against a background of deceit
and scheming, with enough twists in the story to keep us
always on the edge of our seat. The final episodes in Genesis
concern Joseph, a little brat at home, favoured by his father

Jacob, sold into slavery by his jealous brothers, but who rises to the dizzy heights of the Egyptian royal court. This final story of the ancestral history is perhaps the most intriguing and surprising of the lot. Scattered throughout these stories, in both the primaeval and ancestral histories, are genealogies listing the generations of those who lived and died during these times. While at first sight they seem dull in comparison to the great stories, they turn out to be just as captivating.

What is the significance of these two major divisions of Genesis? If the book consisted only of the ancestral history, then one fact would be crystal clear: God is the God of his chosen people Israel. But knowing only that would be misleading. So Genesis includes the primaeval history as an introduction not only to the book itself, but also to the whole Bible. In these chapters we learn that God is not merely the God of Israel, but of all people everywhere – in fact the God of the heavens and the earth. So, at one and the same time, these two 'histories', the primaeval and the ancestral, reveal the greatness of God and invite us to broaden our vision of God's role in our lives.

[1] Many books have been written that deal with these aspects more than adequately. See, for example, C. Mitchell, *Creationism Revisited* (Autumn House, 1999), especially pp. 227-246.

CHAPTER ONE
Fom Chaos to Order
Genesis 1:1-2:4a[2]

The Big Picture

Just as Jesus told apparently simple parables in order to convey deep spiritual truths, so Genesis 1 uses an easily remembered account to help us reflect on matters of first importance. In this way, it is also similar to ancient Near Eastern creation stories. For Israel's neighbours creation was not a self-contained topic, but an opportunity for exploring the crucial questions of human existence, such as 'Who am I?', 'Why am I here?', 'Where am I going?'

The opening words of Genesis, 'In the beginning God created the heavens and the earth' (Gen 1:1), introduce one of the best known chapters in the Bible. Just because it is so familiar, let's pause to take in its broad sweep. Hebrew authors delighted in writing accounts that had a definite design, often using repeated patterns, which they used to underline the significance of what they were writing. The creation account (Gen 1:1-2:4a) is a good example of this. Our appreciation of individual verses is greatly increased if we look at the structure of the whole account. Investigating this structure will also suggest that we should do more than merely read the surface of the story. We have here a narrative working at more than one level. First, note that the account has an introduction (vv. 1-2). The first verse summarises the account that follows, which is concerned with recounting how, 'In the beginning, God created the heavens and the earth' (v. 1). What follows simply fills in the details of this summary. The introduction then continues by describing the state of affairs when God started his work – the earth 'was formless and empty' (v. 2). This phrase translates two Hebrew words, *tōhû wābōhû*. Their exact meaning is debated, but generally they convey the idea of disorder or chaos. That is to say, the world was not yet ordered because God had not yet completed his creative purposes; matter had not yet been shaped, separated and assigned to fulfil God's will.

The second item to note is how the rest of the account describes what God did over the next few days of creation. If we ask the simple question, 'Which new items does God create on each day?', then we get the following simple answers. God first creates light, allowing a distinction to be made between light and darkness, which God calls 'day' and 'night' (vv. 3-5). On the second day, God creates an expanse (or firmament) which acts as a separation between the waters (vv. 6-8). For the moment, we can think of the expanse as being equivalent to our 'sky'. (What this actually represents will be dealt with later.) On the third day, the dry land emerges from the waters and vegetation starts to grow upon it (vv. 9-13). Day four sees the creation of the heavenly bodies, the sun to rule the day and the moon to rule the night, along with the stars (vv. 14-19). On the fifth day God creates animals to inhabit the waters and the air – largely the fish and birds, but not confined to these creatures (vv. 20-23). Land creatures and human beings are created on the sixth day (vv. 24-31). Finally comes the seventh day, on which God adds nothing to his physical creation, but simply rests, blesses and sanctifies (that is, makes holy), the seventh day itself (2:1-3). God's rest on this day is conveyed by the Hebrew verb *šābat*, from which we get our English word Sabbath. Then, to make sure that we have understood what we have just read, the final line echoes the summary with which the account started, 'This is the account of the heavens and the earth when they were created' (Gen 2:4a, compare Gen 1:1).

However, simply summarising the events of each day without seeing how they fit into an overall design, means that we miss much of their significance. When we set out the simple summary outlined above into a diagram, our eyes are opened to a number of matters.

Chaos
(tōhû wābōhû)

Day 1	Day Night	Day 4	Sun Moon/Stars
Day 2	Sea Sky	Day 5	Fish Birds
Day 3	Land Vegetation	Day 6	Land Creatures Humans

Day 7 Rest
(šābat)

The sequence of days in this diagram provides a generally logical progression in creation. For example, the land creatures and humans are not created until there is dry land for them to live on. However, a closer look will show that the creation account has a symmetrical balance between the two columns. So, reading the diagram horizontally, we see that day and night created on day 1 are balanced by day 4 where the sun rules the day, and the moon rules the night (1:16). The sea/waters and sky of day 2 are matched by the fish that live in the waters and the birds that fly in the sky on day 5. Similarly, the land and vegetation created on day 3 are complemented by the land creatures and humans of day 6, both of whom live on the land and are sustained by vegetation (1:29-30). Just as important as these horizontal pairs, however, is the overarching vertical correspondence, between the tōhû wābōhû chaos with which creation starts, and God's šābat, or resting, with which it concludes.

This simple structure underlines some basic affirmations. First, it warns against the common conclusion that human beings are the climax of the account. Quite clearly they are not. The highlight, and the point to which all creation moves, is the blessing and sanctification of the seventh day, the day of šābat/rest. Now why this should be the climax is not explained at this point. It is an issue that Scripture will return to later. But at the very least Genesis wants to tell us that creation cannot be limited to physical objects that can be touched, weighed or photographed. God's blessing, sanctification and *šābat* on the climactic seventh day shows that creation is ultimately a *spiritual* matter.

Secondly, the balance in the structure of the account underlines that God is a God of order. In the same sequence as he creates the 'environments' of days 1-3, so he creates the creatures to live in or rule those 'environments' in days 4-6. Since this is one of the facts about God revealed on the first page of Genesis, we can anticipate that the rest of the book, indeed the rest of Scripture, will have something to say about God's desire for order.

Thirdly, and perhaps most important of all, the creation account shows God bringing order out of chaos. Here we see physical chaos and order, but as Genesis progresses it becomes clear that God also has his eye on moral/spiritual chaos and order. This aspect will be apparent in almost every story we investigate.

However, the overall balance between the days of creation is not the only pattern within the design of the creation story. Even a surface reading of this chapter shows that the account of each day repeats several elements:

a Introduction: 'And God said . . .'
b Command: 'Let there be . . .'; 'Let it be . . .', etc
c Report: 'And it was so'
d Evaluation: 'And God saw that it was good'
e Time framework: 'And there was evening, and there was morning – the X day'

Not only are these elements repeated on each day, but they also occur in the same sequence. So, anyone reading this account settles into a steady rhythm and can predict, to an extent, what will come next. This in itself reveals something about God. The diagram showing the balance between the days of creation indicated that he is a God of order. These elements repeated on each day not only affirm that but also underline how effortless God's creation is. Once God speaks, the elements respond positively. There is no question that God's commands will not be obeyed.

A closer look will show that the pattern of repetition is not absolute, however. There is no evaluation element ('and God saw that it was good'), on the second day. Does this suggest that God created something substandard on that day? No. Once again it probably indicates the importance of repetition and balance in this account. Omitting the evaluation on the second day means that the final emphatic statement on the sixth day, 'God saw all that he had made, *and it was very good*' (1:31), is the *seventh* evaluation in the creation account. For the Hebrews the number seven was important, signifying completeness and wholeness. So, the account is telling us, what God created was absolutely good.

One further observation on the repetition used in the account will underline just how carefully crafted it is. The third and sixth days bring to completion the days of preparation and fulfilment respectively. Each of these days is structured in the same way. They first present the elements of Introduction, Command, Report, and Evaluation (points a-d above), then they repeat that same sequence, before concluding with the final Time Framework. This repetition, unique to these two days, under-lines the fact that each brings its column in the diagram to a climax. Taken as a whole, then, the repetition of this pattern in the first six days is as follows:

		Day 1	*Day 2*	*Day 3*
a	Introduction	v. 3a	v. 6a	vv. 9a, 11a
b	Command	v. 3b	v. 6b	v. 9b, 11b
c	Report	v. 3c	v. 7	vv. 9c, 11c
d	Evaluation	v. 4	xxxxx	vv. 10, 12
e	Time Framework	v. 5	v. 8	vv. 13

		Day 4	*Day 5*	*Day 6*
a	Introduction	v. 14a	v. 20a	vv. 24a, 26a
b	Command	vv. 14b-15a	v. 20b	vv. 24b, 26b
c	Report	v. 15b	v. 21a	vv. 24c, 30b
d	Evaluation	v. 18	v. 21b	vv. 25, 31a
e	Time Framework	v. 19	v. 23	v. 31b

There is ample evidence, therefore, that this account emphasises balance and symmetry. As we have seen, that is important in itself. But often in the biblical text it is the element that breaks the pattern, that stands out as being different, that is the most important of all. That is certainly the case here as well. For the seventh day bucks the trend established by the rest of the account. In the first diagram, set out with two matching columns of three days each, the seventh day is unique. It has no day of creation that corresponds to it. Similarly, it has none of the elements repeated so predictably on all of the other days. It has no introduction, command, report or evaluation. And most tellingly of all, it has no time framework – 'there was evening and there was morning, a seventh day' – as one would have expected, even in the absence of the other elements. The seventh day breaks the pattern. And this is done quite deliberately to underline its significance. The seventh day is blessed. It is also sanctified, or made holy. Nothing else in the whole of creation, according to Genesis, is sanctified. But the seventh day is. Most scholars believe that the basic meaning of the word 'holy', is 'separate', 'set apart'.[3] Genesis emphasises this separation by setting the seventh day apart from the other six by making it depart from the symmetry and balance true of all the other six days.

Once we see the importance of the sanctified seventh day, we can appreciate what might not be immediately obvious. When we first read the account, we might think that the emphasis is on physical items, such as dry land, sun and moon, or on space, such as the expanse/sky. However, while those items are obviously present, something else is stressed just as much, perhaps more. And that is *time*. For example, the account begins with the words, 'In the beginning' (1:1) – an indication of time. The first day, at the head of the first column, sees the creation of light (1:3), which brings the distinction between day and night. This introduces the pattern of evening and morning which regulates the passage of time, from one day to the next. The fourth day, which begins the second column, describes the creation of the heavenly bodies, part of whose function is to 'serve as signs to mark seasons and days and years' (1:14). In other words, they are indicators of time. Then the whole account concludes with the seventh day of God's rest, which is itself made holy. If we map this, using the same basic diagram with which we commenced, we see the following:

Time
('In the beginning')

Day 1:
Time
(Light producing evening/
morning sequence)

Day 4:
Time
(Lights to indicate
seasons/days/years)

Day 2
'evening and morning'

Day 5
'evening and morning'

Day 3
'evening and morning'

Day 6
'evening and morning'

Day 7: Holy Time

Thus the account begins with a statement concerning time. The first column introduces the sequence governing the calculation of time. The second column starts by showing that the heavenly lights will indicate the cycle of time. All six days conclude with an indication of time. And the whole account concludes with holy time. By coming to its climax with holy time, the account shows that there is more to the world than just its physical nuts and bolts.

So, even before the creation account is investigated in any detail, the way in which it is structured indicates some important issues. God is a God of order who brings order out of chaos. He creates every physical object. But the fact that the account concludes with non-physical holy time, shows that God's purposes are not limited to what can be seen by the human eye.

[2] The original biblical documents had no chapter or verse divisions. They were introduced much later as reference aids. The decision on where to place these markers was sometimes unfortunate, as here, where the account concludes half-way through a verse.

[3] E.g. V.P. Hamilton, *The Book of Genesis: Chapters 1-17* (New International Commentary on the Old Testament; ed. R.K. Harrison; Grand Rapids: Eerdmans, 1990), p. 143.

CHAPTER TWO
In More Detail
Genesis 1

*'In the beginning God created the heavens and the earth'
[1:1].*[4]

The opening words of Genesis are so well known that it is
easy to miss just how profound they are. They are breathtaking
in the way they explore the limits of our understanding.

First, they take us to the limits of time – we cannot go back
any further than 'in the beginning'. They also present the limits
of space. The heavens are the highest point above, the earth
the lowest point below. So the phrase 'heavens and earth'
expresses those two extremes and everything in between – a
common Hebrew idiom that expresses the concept of
'everything' (e.g. 1 Chronicles 29:11; Psalm 115:15-16). In other
words, the first thing that Genesis tells us about God is that he
is the lord of time and space.

However, the profundity of this opening verse does not stop
there. Let us look at two points in particular. First, it indicates
that God is eternal, for he was there 'in the beginning'. This
point might seem too obvious to mention. But its significance
becomes clear when we take into account the historical
background to Genesis. In the ancient near east the gods were
not usually considered to be eternal. For example, the
Mesopotamian epic of creation begins with these words:

> When skies above were not yet named
> Nor earth below pronounced by name,
> Apsu, the first one, their begetter
> And maker Tiamat, who bore them all,

Had mixed their waters together,
But had not formed pastures, nor discovered reed-beds;
When yet no gods were manifest,
Nor names pronounced, nor destinies decreed,
Then gods were born within them.[5]

Here then, there is no belief in the eternity of the gods.

The second point to note is that the opening sentence of Genesis makes a clear distinction between God the Creator and his creation. Again, this contrasts with the prevailing view in the ancient world where Genesis was written. There, it was commonly held that there was little if any distinction between the gods and nature, and the gods are often presented as personifications of the natural world. This belief in pantheism was widespread. For example, for the Egyptians, 'each element of the universe was the embodiment of a particular god',[6] while the Mesopotamians 'believed that the gods were totally immanent in nature'.[7]

So, the first verse of Genesis not only reveals a lot about God, but also attacks the common ancient view about religion. In doing this, it sets the trend of the creation account as a whole, which takes every opportunity available to confound the conventional wisdom of its time. In more recent years, the ways in which Genesis disagrees with modern humanistic atheism have been emphasised. The assumption has often been that as an ancient work, Genesis simply reflects the general views of its own time. This is not the case. Genesis has always been out of step, not only with the prevailing views of its own time, but also with ours today. It was radical then. It is radical now.

Having told us that God created the heavens and the earth, verse 2 turns its attention to the *earth*. In fact, the Hebrew could be translated as, 'Now as far as the earth was concerned, it was formless and empty (*tōhû wābōhû*)'. An exact translation is difficult because this combination of words, *tōhû wābōhû*, is found in only one other place in the Bible (Jeremiah 4:23). But if we look at its use there, and the context of Gen 1:2, then it is probable that 'chaos' or 'disorder' is intended. 'The cosmos was empty of purpose, meaning and function, a place that had no order or intelligibility.'[8] That was the condition of the earth when God first started his creative act.

Also present, along with the chaos and darkness, is 'the Spirit of God' (v. 2). Christian readers of Genesis cannot help but make a connection between this statement and the New Testament revelation of the Trinity – Father, Son and Holy Spirit. But we should be cautious about reading every New Testament doctrine into Old Testament texts. The Hebrew term translated as 'Spirit' here is *rûah*. The word is ambiguous, just as the New Testament Greek equivalent *pneuma* is. Both words can also be translated as 'wind' or 'breath'. Interestingly, in Gen 8:1, in the middle of the flood story, there is a situation that is identical to the one described here. There, as here, the earth is covered with water, and the *rûah* of God is moving over its surface. But while in Gen 1:2 *rûah* is usually translated as 'spirit', in Gen 8:1 all English versions translate it as 'wind'. So, we should be careful about insisting that *rûah* in Gen 1:2 presents the doctrine of the Trinity. The text is clear that God is present and that he is creating, but it is not making any explicit doctrinal statement about the Trinity.

The first day (1:3-5), begins with the words, 'And God said'. But to whom was God speaking? There is no other being present to carry out God's command. Yet all he does is speak, and his will is obeyed, showing that he has control over matter. He creates effortlessly, through the power of his word. This is in sharp contrast, once again, to beliefs about creation in the ancient world. Then, it was generally believed that creation was the result of a great struggle. For example, the Babylonian creation epic describes how the great god Marduk battles with Tiamat, the great female monster of the deep:

> [Marduk] shot an arrow which pierced her belly,
> Split her down the middle and slit her heart,
> Vanquished her and extinguished her life.
> He threw down her corpse and stood on top of her.[9]

So, Genesis takes issue with the received wisdom of its time. And, incidentally, this forms part of the background to the introduction to John's gospel. Just as in Genesis God spoke his word and creation came forth, so 'In the beginning was the Word, and the Word was with God, and the Word was God' (John 1:1). This Word of God, present at creation, is also central in re-creation. For 'the Word became flesh and made his dwelling among us' (John 1:14). God is the God of re-creation because first he was the God of creation.

As well as creating, God names what he creates – but not everything. On the first day God names 'day' and 'night' (v. 5), on the second, 'sky' (v. 8), and on the third 'land' and 'seas' (v. 10). These are the only parts of his creation that he names: the basic elements of time ('day' and 'night') and space ('sky', 'land' and 'seas'). Giving names and assigning functions are prerogatives of an overlord. In other words, God is the lord of time and space, just as we saw in the account's opening verse.

The second day of creation (1:6-8), probably raises more questions for the modern reader than any other. We have difficulties visualising what the 'expanse' or 'firmament' actually is, and how it 'separates water from water', and what exactly the 'water above' and 'water beneath' it are.

There have been a number of suggestions. Some think that the 'expanse' is the atmosphere, and the 'water beneath' is the seas, rivers and oceans. The 'water above' in this scenario is either the clouds, or a canopy of water which in the beginning encircled the earth. In the time of Noah, it is suggested, this large body of water collapsed, causing the great deluge, and so no longer exists.

There are, however, some problems with this view. First, the Bible is clear that the waters above the expanse are still there. For example, Psalm 148:4 says, 'Praise him, you highest heavens and you waters above the skies.' For this psalmist, therefore, the 'waters above' were certainly not a temporary feature that disappeared at the time of Noah, for he calls on them in his time, poetically, to praise God.

Also, the Bible refers to the 'expanse' in other places, for example in Job 37:18, 'can you join him in spreading out the skies, hard as a mirror of cast bronze?' In antiquity mirrors were made from highly polished metal. So, strangely to our modern minds, the skies (expanse, firmament) are spoken of as being a hard object that could be touched. If we now look back at the details in Genesis 1 then matters get even more intriguing. Concerning the expanse/firmament the account tells us that there is water *under* it and *above* it (1:7); the sun and moon are *in* it (1:14, 17), and the birds fly *across* it (1:20).

It is very difficult, if not impossible, to reconcile this description with modern notions about the structure of the world. For example, it suggests that the waters *above* the expanse are even higher than the sun and moon, which are merely *in* it. However, while this description causes problems for our modern mind, it would not have been a problem for ancient people. There were many different views in the ancient near east concerning the structure of the universe, or cosmology as it is technically called. Egypt and Mesopotamia each had several.[10] The picture painted in Genesis 1 does not conform entirely to any of these, but its central features were commonly held: a firmament above, in which the heavenly bodies were set, with waters above and below this firmament, as well as under the earth.[11]

It would appear, therefore, that Genesis simply utilises some of the common cosmological views of the ancient world. At first sight this might seem to contradict an important point that I've made previously, that is, that the creation account counters the commonly held beliefs of its time. We should note carefully, however, what Genesis opposes and what it does not. It challenges the *theological*, but not the *cosmological* views of Israel's neighbours. An ancient person who read Genesis 1 would not have been surprised by its cosmology, but would have been scandalised by its theology. This gives us an important insight into the purpose of the account. In the grand scheme of things it matters little what one's views on astronomy and cosmology are. What is absolutely critical is that we understand the truth about God and how he relates to us. This is what Genesis wants us to see, without getting on to sidetracks concerning light years, elliptical orbits or parsecs. It uses commonly held ancient cosmological views as a vehicle to convey theological truths to its original readers. In the same way, Jesus used popular concepts of his time to convey the truth of the gospel (e.g. Luke 16:19-31).

On the third day (1:9-13), the environment appears in which human beings will eventually live, with the separation of the dry land from the seas. A new aspect of God's creation that emerges on this day is fertility. The dry land itself is commanded to produce vegetation, which in turn has the power of procreation in the seed within its fruit. The phrase 'the land *produced* vegetation' (1:12), is revealing. The same verb is used for a mother (e.g. Gen 25:26; Job 1:21), or father (e.g. Gen 46:26), producing a child. Fertility and reproduction is a gift that God gives throughout his creation. He did not create this world as a desert. The richness of his world is conveyed by the phrase 'according to their kinds' (v. 12). These words have often been misinterpreted to support the notion of the fixity of species. That is, God created the various species of plants, or animals (vv. 21, 25), and they were only able to reproduce 'after their kinds'. This argument has been used in the sometimes acrimonious debates over creation and evolution, and the impossibility of one species evolving into another. This is not the point here. 'After their kinds' is simply a Hebrew phrase that refers to the variety of species, and could equally well be translated as 'of every kind', as it is by NRSV. The point at issue here is the variety and richness of creation, not an argument against evolution.

The account of the fourth day (1:14-19), in which the heavenly bodies are created, is the longest so far. The reason for this is that it details the functions of these luminaries. They are 'to separate the day from the night' (v. 14) and 'light from darkness' (v. 18); 'to give light on the earth' (vv. 15, 17); the sun is 'to govern the day', and the moon 'to govern the night' (v. 16); they also 'serve as signs to mark seasons and days and years' (v. 14). The reason why the account is preoccupied with stating their function is once again found in the religious views of the time. The book has already said plenty to shock an ancient reader about the nature and acts of God. But what would startle such a reader here is not so much what the text says, but what it does not say. Generally, the heavenly bodies were believed to be gods who ruled human destinies according to their appearance or position in the sky, as the following passage illustrates:

When a halo surrounds the Moon and Jupiter stands within it, the King of Akkad will be besieged. When a halo surrounds the Moon and Jupiter stands within it, there will be a slaughter of cattle and beasts of the field. . . . When a halo surrounds the Moon and Scorpio stands in it, it will cause men to marry princesses, (or) lions will die, and the traffic of the land will be hindered. . . . When a halo surrounds the Moon, and Regulus stands within it, women will bear male children.[12]

Genesis attacks this view head on. It limits the functions of the sun, moon and stars to separating and governing the day and night, shedding light on the earth and indicating seasons, days and years. They have no role in human destiny at all, because they are not gods, but simply lights. So, implicitly the account is inviting its readers to reject any form of sun or moon worship, and all forms of astrology that claim to predict the future of individuals based on their sign of the zodiac. It rejects a fatalistic view of human existence.

This significant point is driven home by two other features. First, many readers of Genesis are puzzled as to why God creates light on the first day but creates the heavenly luminaries only on the fourth day. Actually, this is neither an oversight nor a problem. On the first day the word 'light' is used five times. On the corresponding fourth day, the word 'lights' is used five times. Through this repetition the text underlines the connection between the two days in order to say something significant about God and the heavenly bodies: God is the source of light. The heavenly bodies are simply the means he chooses later to fulfil that role. In other words, worship God the source of light, not the sun, moon or stars that are part of his creation. To make this point even clearer, note how the account does not use the words 'sun' or 'moon' to describe what God created. Rather, it uses the terms 'the greater light' and 'the lesser light'. Apparently, Genesis does this so that there can be no ambiguity at all that the heavenly bodies are not to be worshipped. For the Hebrew words for 'sun' and 'moon' were also the names of the sun-god and moon-goddess in some ancient near eastern languages.[13] So it does not even use these words in case there is any misunderstanding. For similar reasons, the 'stars' are placed last after sun and moon, almost as an afterthought, because they were usually accorded pride of place in astrological texts.[14]

Genesis is adamant. The heavenly lights are merely lights, placed there by God to fulfil certain functions. But since they are merely lights, their function is not to control or indicate human destiny. That lies in the hand of God, the creator of 'the heavens and the earth'. This point is made more explicit elsewhere, for example when God judges any Israelite who, 'contrary to my command has worshipped other gods, bowing down to them or to the sun or the moon or the stars of the sky' (Deuteronomy 17:3). The wisdom of Genesis might be just as offensive to modern readers as it was to its ancient ones. To those who view astrology as giving valid insights into their personal destinies, the account asserts that the heavenly bodies are lights, and nothing more. On the other hand, to those who view the universe as being run merely by the 'laws of physics', the account points to the creator God, who transcends physical laws.

Most English translations render the end of 1:16 as 'he also made the stars' (e.g. NIV), or similar. One commonly hears that this statement is parenthetical, that is, it affirms that God made the stars, but does not indicate when he did so. The stars could have been there for millions of years. As appealing as this interpretation is to those whose main aim in reading Genesis is to address scientific questions, it is very unlikely. Most commentators, of all persuasions, are in agreement on this. The argument is too technical to go into here, but those wishing to pursue it may refer to more detailed volumes.[15] One also sometimes hears it confidently asserted that the Hebrew word for 'made' ('āsâ), can mean 'revealed', and that the heavenly bodies, in existence for a long time, were simply unveiled on the fourth day. There are no grounds whatsoever for this interpretation.[16] In any case, the same verb is used ten times in the creation account. Why does it mean 'reveal' only on the fourth day? The only motivation for this suggestion is to harmonise the Bible with preconceived views on astronomy or cosmology. This account might well cause problems for a modern reader who understands it to be an accurate scientific document, and who also believes that modern science is correct. But remember, the account caused problems for its ancient readers as well.

On the fifth day (1:20-23), God creates the creatures of the waters and the air. Just as on the third day where the land 'produced' vegetation (1:12), so here the land 'produces' living creatures (1:24). We are reminded again of the fertility that God builds into his world. This essential element in God's creation is further highlighted when he blesses the creatures that appear on this day. Nothing so far has been blessed. And it is good for modern readers to note that while 'blessing' can be fairly abstract for us, it is almost always concrete for the writers of the Old Testament. The content of God's blessing here is sexual reproduction. This is no minor issue, for the goodness of sexuality, and its place in God's design, will be picked up later on the next day of creation (1:28), and explored in the chapters that follow.

Another aspect of this day is illuminated by reading with one eye on ancient mythologies. Egyptian and Mesopotamian texts describe how sea monsters had to be overcome before the creation of the cosmos. In Old Testament poetic texts the term *tannîn*, used here for 'creatures of the sea' (1:21), is used in tandem with Rahab and Leviathan, monstrous beasts overpowered by God (Psalm 74:13; Isaiah 27:1; 51:9). In these highly metaphorical biblical texts the term *tannîn* carries the same connotation as in the myths of Israel's neighbours. Yet here, in the creation account, it refers simply to the sea creatures created by God, underlining the effortless creation of God rather than a battle between foes.[17]

The account of the sixth day, on which land animals and human beings are created, is the most detailed. This is due to the fact that the text wants to make clear the relationships between human beings and the animals, on the one hand, and with God on the other.

Animals and human beings have a great deal in common. They are both created on the same day. They both live in the same environment, dry land (vv. 24, 28), and have the same food, plants (vv. 29-30). But, just as clearly, human beings are not simply animals. They are God's representatives on earth, for they were created 'in the image of God' (v. 27). We have seen how Genesis has disagreed with the received wisdom of its own time. Here, quite clearly, it disagrees with the assumptions of atheistic humanism of our time. Genesis affirms that we have many similarities with the animals, but we are not just another species of mammal. Our unique relationship to God makes us more than that.

Genesis 1:26 is crucial for understanding what human beings are, and our relationship to God: 'Then God said, "Let us make man in our image, in our likeness, and let them rule over the fish of the sea and the birds of the air, over the livestock, over all the earth, and over all the creatures that move along the ground."'

God's use of the plural 'Let *us* . . .', has intrigued readers for centuries. Why does he not say, 'Let *me* . . .'? Many suggestions have been made. For example, some suggest that God is addressing the angels. But since the angels are created beings themselves, it is unlikely that God is requesting their help. Others suggest that God's command is an example of the 'royal plural'. So, just as Queen Victoria famously announced that '*we* are not amused', when she was referring only to herself, so God uses the same idiom. Unfortunately, while this explanation would work with English, or some other modern languages, it does not work with Hebrew. There are no examples of the 'royal plural' anywhere else in the Old Testament.[18]

Another common suggestion, made by sincere Christians, is that the plural demonstrates the Trinity. We have already mentioned the difficulty in reading the New Testament doctrine of the Trinity into the text of Genesis when looking at the use of *rûah* (wind/spirit), in 1:2. Without denying that the doctrine of the Trinity is a model that does justice to all of the New Testament material, it is unlikely that the Trinity is revealed in Genesis 1:26. First of all, the use of the plural 'us' does not in itself demonstrate the threefold nature of God. From the use of the simple plural, one could just as easily argue for twofold or ninefold. Secondly, the most important objection to this and all of the other suggestions is, why is the plural used in verse 26 *and nowhere else in Genesis 1*? That is to say, if the plural refers to the angels, the royal plural, or the Trinity, one would expect it to be used throughout the chapter and not just in one verse.

The most likely explanation is that the plural is an example of the 'plural of deliberation'. A number of scholars have observed that Hebrew sometimes switches from the singular to the plural in order to underline the significance of what is being said.[19] For example, in the story of Babel as a whole, God's actions are expressed through singular verbs. The one exception is when God says, 'Come, *let us* go down and confuse their language so they will not understand each other.' He cannot be referring to the angels, because in the next verse the Lord alone goes down. 'So the Lord scattered them from there over all the earth, and they stopped building the city' (11:8). In this example of the 'plural of deliberation', the use of 'let us' underlines just how important and solemn God's action is. The confusion of language and the scattering of people groups affects the rest of human history.

So now we can see the probable significance of God's command, 'Let *us* make man in our image' (1:26). God has created the whole of the physical creation, from light on the first day to animals on the sixth, and now he turns to his final creation – human beings, uniquely created in the image of God. The plural is used in the command in order to emphasise just how important human beings are in the grand scheme of God's creation.

Just how significant we are is shown by the fact that in the whole of creation only human beings are made in the image of God. What exactly that means has again been debated widely. However, at the very least it means that we have a capacity to have a relationship with God. In this we are unlike any other creature in God's world. The account, however, suggests some more possibilities. 'Then God said, "Let us make man in our image, in our likeness, *and let them rule over* the fish of the sea and the birds of the air, over the livestock, over all the earth, and over all the creatures that move along the ground"' (1:26). This verse suggests that our rule over the animals is part of what it means to be in the image of God. In this way we reflect something of God. For God has just demonstrated his dominion over creation by speaking it into existence. He now hands over part of that dominion to human beings, just as previously he handed over responsibility for light to the heavenly bodies on the fourth day. Seen in this way, being in the image of God refers not only to what we *are* but also to what we *do*. We represent God on earth. Ancient kings would erect images of themselves in parts of their empire where they were not present. Such images represented the authority of the king. In the same way, any authority humans have in the world is derived from God, not from their own inherent power.

Once again, this view of humanity is radically different from that of many cultures in the ancient world. For these people human beings were usually insignificant elements in creation. 'They possessed little dignity and worth and were thought to be merely slaves of the gods.'[20] But in Genesis human beings are God's representatives on earth, given a divine mandate to rule God's world. This is a liberation from the fatalism of many ancients. However, we must understand the context of Genesis before we simply apply the idea of human dominion over nature to our own time. In Genesis, human beings are God's representatives, so they must exercise dominion as God would. They have a responsibility to represent God, not merely to act in whatever way they wish. Seen in this light, giving humans dominion over nature spells out our responsibilities as much as our rights. It certainly gives us no license to exploit God's world and its resources for our own selfish ends.

This account of creation concludes with the seventh day (2:1-3). A literal rendering of its opening words would be, 'Thus the heavens and the earth were finished . . . And on the seventh day God finished the work' (Gen 2:1-2a). Not surprisingly this has puzzled some readers, for it seems to say that God had finished what he was doing and then he proceeded to finish it![21] So had he finished or not? The ancient Greek translation, the Septuagint, gets around the problem by translating Genesis 2:2a as, 'And God finished on the *sixth day* his works . . .' This radical but totally unwarranted translation, substituting 'sixth' for 'seventh', also protects God from accusations that he broke the Sabbath by working on it!

However, a close look at the text shows that the problem is only imagined. By the end of the sixth day God had indeed completed his creation of the physical universe. That is why Genesis 2:1, at the beginning of the seventh day, says that 'the heavens and the earth were finished'. All *physical* things, 'the heavens and the earth', those things that can be seen, touched, smelt, heard and tasted – they are certainly 'finished'. But God's work is not yet finished. That is only achieved when God blesses and sanctifies the seventh day. This holy seventh day is not part of the heavens and earth that can be comprehended by the senses. Holy time is a spiritual, not a physical matter. It can only be experienced, not observed. By concluding with God resting, blessing and sanctifying, the account makes it clear that any view of the world that excludes the spiritual is totally inadequate. Without that, God's work would not be 'finished'.

The significance of this seventh day of holy rest is not spelled out in detail at this point. But enough is said to anticipate what the rest of Scripture says.[22] On days 1-3, God names his creation. On days 5 and 6 he blesses it. But on the seventh day he both blesses and sanctifies the day itself. By contrast, no physical object in the 'heavens and earth' is sanctified, not even human beings who were created in the image of God. Why should the seventh day be distinguished like this? It is God's final act of separation. Previously God had separated the light from the darkness (1:4); waters above from waters beneath (1:7); dry land from seas (1:9-10). He now separates the seventh day from all other days, setting it apart for holy use. All days are God's days, but this day is God's day *par excellence*, advertising that the heartbeat of God's creation is blessing, holiness and spirituality.

Our understanding of Genesis 1 has been illuminated by ancient near eastern mythology, and the description of the seventh day is no exception. In several ancient creation myths the gods desire a resting place. So, for example, in the Babylonian creation myth the god Marduk creates a shrine as his place of rest in the sacred city of Babylon. The imagery of the temple as God's resting place is also picked up in the Old Testament, 'For the Lord has chosen Zion, he has desired it for his dwelling: "This is my resting place for ever and ever"' (Psalm 132:13-14). Seen in this context, therefore,

This seventh day is not a theological appendix to the creation account, just to bring closure now that the main event of creating people has been reported. Rather, it intimates the purpose of creation and of the cosmos. God does not set up the cosmos so that only people will have a place. He also sets up the cosmos to serve as his temple in which he will find rest in the order and equilibrium that he has established.[23]

When we look back on this first account in Scripture, we see that it paints a fascinating portrait of God and his ways in the world. It is all the more fascinating because it avoids many questions which we often think are the most important. It conceals more than it reveals. But what it reveals is what Genesis considers important. As a preface to the book of Genesis it provides an orientation to the world for the believing reader. In order to live in this world with understanding, we must first understand not so much the world itself, but the God who created it.

Its picture of God is clearly painted from the point of view of human beings and this earth. Yet it warns us against taking too narrow a view of God. In the ancestral history (chapters 12-50), God is primarily the God of the chosen people. Prior to that, in the primaeval history as a whole (chs. 1-11), it is clear that God is the God of all people. But right at the outset, the creation account demonstrates that he is the God of all creation, human and non-human alike. 'A god who is understood only as the god of humankind is no longer the God of the Bible.'[24]

Among many other matters, Genesis 1 makes clear that whatever exists was created by God, effortlessly. He is the eternal God of order who brings order out of chaos. He is the lord of time and space, who has control over matter, making a fertile and richly varied world. He creates human beings with whom he can have a relationship, whose destiny is in his hands and not decided by the random position of the sun, moon or stars. And he concludes his creation with holy Sabbath rest, building it into the rhythm of history, to indicate that life needs spiritual nurture if it is to be lived as God intended it.

All in all, therefore, Genesis tells us that this world had a meaningful beginning. If there is no meaningful beginning, there can be no meaningful end. And if there is neither a meaningful beginning nor end, *then there is no meaningful present*. Genesis 1 counters this bleak pessimism by assuring us that the world and human existence are more than the end result of a cosmic accident. The creation story gives us understanding of the past, hope for the future, and meaning for the present.

[4] Some modern versions translate this verse not as a separate sentence, but as part of a longer one, e.g. 'In the beginning when God created the heavens and the earth, the earth was a formless void . . .' (NRSV). The linguistic issues are too complicated to go into here. However, while such a translation is possible, it is not, in my opinion, the most likely one. Regardless of how one translates, the major points I make in my comments are not affected.

[5] S. Dalley, *Myths from Mesopotamia: Creation, the Flood, Gilgamesh, and Others* (Revised; Oxford: Oxford University Press, 2000), p. 233. (Ital. sup.).

[6] J.D. Currid, *Ancient Egypt and the Old Testament* (Grand Rapids: Baker Books, 1997), p. 35.

[7] Currid, *Ancient Egypt*, p. 38.

[8] J.H. Walton, 'Creation', in T. Desmond Alexander and David W. Baker (eds.), *Dictionary of the Old Testament: Pentateuch* (Downers Grove/Leicester: InterVarsity Press, 2003), p. 157.

[9] Dalley, *Myths*, p. 253.

[10] Currid, *Ancient Egypt*, pp. 33-49.

[11] E.C. Lucas, 'Cosmology', in T. Desmond Alexander and David W. Baker (eds.), *Dictionary of the Old Testament: Pentateuch* (Downers Grove/Leicester: InterVarsity Press, 2003), pp. 130-9; Walton, 'Creation', pp. 155-68.

[12] From R.C. Thompson, 'The Reports of the Magicians and Astrologers of Nineveh and Babylon', in R.F. Harper (ed.), *Assyrian and Babylonian Literature: Selected Transactions with a Critical Introduction* (New York: Appleton, 1904).

[13] See *Hebrew and Aramaic Lexicon of the Old Testament* (ed. L. Koehler and W. Baumgartner; Leiden: Brill Academic Publishers, 2002).

[14] See e.g. Tablet V in Dalley, *Myths*, pp. 255-6.

[15] For example, J. H. Sailhamer, *The Pentateuch as Narrative: A Biblical-Theological Commentary* (Grand Rapids: Zondervan, 1992), pp. 92, 3.

[16] The verb 'āsâ is not present in the clause 'he also made the stars', but is used for God's making the sun and moon. The verbless clause regarding the stars assumes the same verb. Nevertheless, there are no examples anywhere in the Old Testament of the Hebrew verb 'āsâ meaning 'reveal'. See *HALOT*. If the text had intended us to understand that the heavenly bodies were merely revealed, one would have expected some form of the verbs glh, 'tr or r'h.

[17] See Walton, 'Creation', p. 160.

[18] The only possible example is Ezra 4:18, but this is written in Aramaic, not Hebrew. Even here, the use of the idiom is not certain.

[19] For example, C. Westermann (1974), *Genesis 1-11: A Commentary* (trans. J. J. Scullion; Minneapolis: Augsburg Publishing House, 1984), p. 145.

[20] Currid, *Ancient Egypt*, p. 48. See also Lucas, 'Cosmology', p. 165.

[21] The New International Version overcomes the apparent contradiction by translating the beginning of Gen 2:2 as a pluperfect, e.g. '*By* the seventh day God *had* finished the work . . .' While this is possible grammatically, it misses the important point the text conveys.

[22] For example, see Exodus 16:23-30; 20:8-11; 31:14-16; Leviticus 23:3; Deuteronomy 5:12-14; Isaiah 56:2, 6; 58:13.

[23] Walton, 'Creation', p. 161.

[24] Westermann, *Genesis 1-11*, p. 176.

CHAPTER THREE
The God Who is Near
Genesis 2

We've already seen that when asked to talk about really important issues an ancient Hebrew would often reply, 'Let me tell you a story'. Creation is so significant that Genesis now says, 'Let me tell you another story'. A single account cannot do justice to the topic.

This second account, beginning in Genesis 2:4b, is quite different. The contrasts with the first are often paraded as if they pose a problem. This might seem so at first sight, to a western mind, but clearly not to the ancient Hebrews. Western education and logic reflects classical Greek thinking. So, we tend to look at an issue with all of its complexity, and then provide an answer that synthesises the data into a single elegant explanation.

The Hebrew mind often approached matters differently, saying of a complex issue, 'It's like this – but it's also like this'. That is why we sometimes find seemingly contradictory statements placed side by side. For example, two successive verses read, 'Do not answer a fool according to his folly, or you will be like him yourself. Answer a fool according to his folly, or he will be wise in his own eyes' (Proverbs 26:4-5). Putting these proverbs next to each other shows us that there is no single way to deal with a fool. It depends on the kind of fool you are dealing with. And there's more than one way of describing creation, as Genesis 1, 2 demonstrate. Just as the four gospels in the New Testament provide four different portraits of Jesus, sometimes telling events in his life in a different sequence, so too Genesis presents two renditions of creation.

These two stories must not be read independently, however. They have a close connection, and a hint of this is suggested by the way in which the first ends and the second begins. The final line of the first story, 'This is the account of the heavens and the earth when they were created' (2:4a), contains the three key terms 'heavens', 'earth' and 'created'. The first line of the next story, 'When the Lord God made the earth and the heavens' (2:4b), echoes these same elements, but notice the arrangement:

	A	B	C
2:4a	'heavens'	'earth'	'created'
2:4b	'made'	'earth'	'heavens'
	C	B	A

The main elements of 2:4a, ABC, are repeated in reverse order, CBA, in 2:4b, an arrangement known as a chiasm. The reversal of the normal sequence heavens-earth (2:4a), to earth-heavens (2:4b), is particularly striking.[25] The chiasm is a way of integrating the conclusion and introduction of the two stories in order to indicate that they need to be read together, as complementary accounts.

First of all, the stories differ concerning the role of humanity. In Genesis 1, the creation of the physical world builds up to its climax on the sixth day with the creation of human beings. In Genesis 2, their significance is expressed in a different way. Here they are placed not at the end, but at the centre, as the pivot on which the whole story turns. The second major difference is that the events are told in a different sequence in the second story. For example, the order of God's creating vegetation, animals and humans is as follows:

Chapter 1
a) vegetation (vv. 11-12)
b) land animals (vv. 24-25)
c) humans (male/female) (vv. 24-27)

Chapter 2
a) male human (v. 7)
b) vegetation (v. 9)
c) land animals (v. 19)
d) female human (vv. 21, 22)

These differences are not a problem, but as we shall see, an opportunity to gain a different perspective on God and the world he creates.

The major new perspective we gain from the second story is its portrait of God, especially about the way he relates to us.

In chapter1 two nouns were stressed when God created humans. They were created in God's *image*, after his *likeness*.

Chapter 2 emphasises two verbs: God *formed* the man from the dust, and *breathed* into his nostrils the breath of life (2:7). This gives us a radically different insight into the nature of God. The first account presents him as the almighty creator, totally in control, who has only to speak and the elements obey his will. This aspect of God is celebrated elsewhere in Scripture. For example, 'By the word of the Lord were the heavens made, their starry host by the breath of his mouth' (Psalm 33:6).

But knowing that much about God is not enough. In fact it could be dangerously misleading to see only the transcendence of God, for by itself it might suggest that he is somewhat impersonal and distant. So, the second creation account balances the portrait of God by painting him as being intimately and lovingly involved in creation. He 'formed' the man from the dust of the ground. The Hebrew word comes from a root used to describe a potter who forms a vessel from a lump of clay on his wheel (Jeremiah 18:4), or of a skilled artisan shaping a piece of metal (Isaiah 44:12). So when God 'forms' a man he is not standing at a distance, speaking him into existence, but intimately involved in his creation, as any skilled craftsman would be. To emphasise this side of his personality, he also 'breathed into his nostrils the breath of life'. This conjures up the image of an embrace, a closeness that amounts to a 'kiss of life' from the creator.

The intimacy between God and Man in this account contrasts with, but does not contradict, the transcendence of the almighty God in Genesis 1. Neither portrait exhausts what God is, for he is both. This is affirmed throughout Scripture. For example, Isaiah says, 'For this is what the high and lofty One says – he who lives for ever, whose name is holy: "I live in a high and holy place, but also with him who is contrite and lowly in spirit, to revive the spirit of the lowly and to revive the heart of the contrite"' (Isaiah 57:15). The high and holy God also relates to us as individuals.

So, how exactly does God relate to the creature he has just created? We must be careful to read everything that God does. He first indicates what the Man's purpose in life will be, 'The Lord God took the man and put him in the Garden of Eden to work it and take care of it' (2:15). The Man will find his fulfilment in working in and caring for the environment God has prepared for him. Secondly, he gives him a life of freedom, telling him, ' "You are free to eat from any tree in the garden" ' (2:16). But, as the third point shows, God did not give him absolute freedom: ' "but you must not eat from the tree of the knowledge of good and evil, for when you eat of it you will surely die" ' (2:17).

It is important to see all three of these points. In some popular readings of this story it is commonly said that God's first words to the Man are a prohibition. God hems the Man in, stifling his freedom and creativity. A moment's pause will confirm that this misrepresents God. God gives the Man *three* things: a fulfilling vocation in working in the garden; broad freedom in being able to eat from the trees in the garden; and *one* prohibition – he may not eat from one tree, for if he does, he will die.

How God relates to the first human is a model for how God relates to all of us. God gives each one of us various talents and differing vocations.[26] He also allows us a great degree of freedom, for he has given each one of us the freedom of choice. But the single prohibition he gave to the Man in the garden reminds us of a truth of human existence: absolute freedom is no blessing. History is full of examples of individuals who amassed such great personal power that they were free to act as they wished. One is hard pressed to find any one of them who was a blessing to the world.

The punishment for disobedience is clear and stark. Eating from the tree of the knowledge of good and evil will result in a death sentence. In the garden, therefore, there is not only a tree of life, but also a tree of death. We must be careful not to run ahead of where we are in the story so far, knowing what happens when the human couple do eat from the tree. Some who do this manipulate what God actually said. So, one often hears, the Hebrew text actually says, 'when you eat of it, *dying you will die*'. That is, you will begin to die as soon as you eat the fruit, and as time progresses your life force will diminish until eventually you will be dead.

Unfortunately, this misunderstands the Hebrew idiom being used.

It is true that the grammatical construction, taken literally, could be translated this way. But numerous examples of the construction in the Old Testament indicate clearly that it is used in order to make an emphatic statement.[27] So, we could translate, 'when you eat of it, *you will certainly die*'. For example, exactly the same words were said to Jeremiah after he presented his controversial sermon in the Jerusalem temple. 'The priests, the prophets and all the people seized him and said, "*You must die!*"' (Jeremiah 26:8)[28] They clearly had no long drawn out event in mind. For the moment, therefore, in this story, we know that a death sentence hangs over the one who disobeys. What actually happens, and why, we will investigate in chapter 3.

The climax of chapter 2 is the creation of the Woman. Her arrival is a good example of how the contrasts between chapters 1 and 2 enrich our understanding. A refrain throughout chapter 1 was God's evaluation of creation – 'it was good' (1:4, 10, 12, 18, 21, 25), culminating in 'it was very good' (1:31). In a startling reversal of fortune we now read, 'It is not good' (2:18). What is not good is that the Man is alone. When God first created humanity, therefore, he created us as social beings. He designed us to share our lives with other people. To live our lives in isolation from others, or to emphasise our individual rights rather than our responsibilities to others, 'is not good'. How God goes about solving the Man's problem of being alone is unusual, if not to say amusing. He announces that he will 'make a helper suitable for him' (2:18). What sort of helper does the Man need? First of all, he needs help to fulfil God's blessings given in 1:28, ' "Be fruitful and increase in number; fill the earth and subdue it. Rule over the fish of the sea and the birds of the air and over every living creature that moves on the ground." ' At the very least, the Man by himself cannot reproduce, fill the earth and subdue it! Ruling over the entire animal creation would be a challenge for an individual as well. He also needs help in his vocation to work in and care for the garden (2:15). In short, he needs help to be a fulfilled human being. He cannot achieve this in isolation.

We are taken by surprise, therefore, when God proceeds to create animals, and brings these to the Man.[29] We already saw how chapter 1 affirmed the similarities between humans and animals, yet at the same time underlined their differences (see comments on 1:24-31). This account does the same in its own way. Just as God had formed the Man from the dust of the ground (2:7), he now forms creatures and birds from the ground (2:19).

The Man shares a common origin with the animals. Yet they are clearly different, for the Man gives names to all of them (2:20a), demonstrating his dominion announced in chapter 1. And the greatest difference is that among the huge array of creatures paraded before the Man and named by him, not a single one is suitable as his 'helper' (2:20b). Not one. No matter how much the Man is impressed by the dromedary, tree frog, three-toed sloth or bristle-thighed curlew, he knows that none of these can fulfil his need for a partner with whom to share his life. If for no other reason, no helper can be found among the animals because he needs a helper to have dominion over the animals.

But that isn't the only reason, of course. One might wonder why it takes so long to provide the Man with his true helper. The delay is surely not due to the fact that God does not know what he is doing. Rather, the frustration in not finding his true partner underlines for the Man just how important she is once she does arrive. That is demonstrated by the Man's response to God's next move. God performs an operation on the Man, removing one of his ribs and makes this into a woman (2:22). God shows the same intimate creative design here as when he 'formed' the Man as a potter would. Literally, the text says that he 'built' the rib into a woman, as a builder would. And as soon as the Man sees this wonderful creature, he cries out, 'This is now bone of my bones and flesh of my flesh' (2:23).

However, this conventional translation does not convey the deep emotion. It is better conveyed as 'At last/finally! . . .'[30] The pent up frustration is released. The Man has never seen a woman before, but he knows intuitively, with no need for prompting, that she is what he has been looking for. When he was alone, it was 'not good'. But now she has arrived, this is definitely good!

We have had ample evidence of the intimacy between God and his creation. Now, the intimacy between the Man and Woman is emphasised. The exclamation, 'bone of my bones and flesh of my flesh', can be read at two levels. The Woman, having come from his side, is quite literally part of his flesh and bone. But the words are also a Hebrew idiom expressing deep intimacy and relationship. So, for example, similar words are used by Laban to describe his closeness to his nephew Jacob (Gen. 29:14) and by the Israelite tribes in their commitment to King David (2 Samuel 5:1). The naming of the Woman contains a play on words which also underlines intimacy: 'she shall be called "woman" (iššâ), for she was taken out of man (îš)' (2:23).

A common Hebrew technique is to point out significance by using wordplay. There was a similar case when the Man ('ādām, using a different word on this occasion), was formed from the ground ('ᵃdāmâ), showing how closely these two are related (2:7). What is more, the Man has come as close as any man ever will to giving birth. The Woman has come from within him. And as a mother adores the child she has borne, so the Man cherishes the Woman.

Without sentimentalising the relationship between the two, the text underlines their intimacy with two further images. The two 'will become one flesh' (2:24), not in the mundane sense of simply having children, as some have suggested, but sexually, spiritually and in every way united. They were also naked, but 'they felt no shame' (2:25). That is to say, there were no barriers, no self-consciousness or embarrassment. They were simply at home in each other's company.

Once again, looking at the contrasts between the two creation stories, this time at the way they conclude, enhances our understanding. The first account of creation concluded with holy Sabbath rest on the seventh day. The significance of this was not explained, but it was clear that the creation of blessed and holy time transcends the physical universe. So the first account reminds us of our relationship with God.

The second creation account concludes with the intimate relationships between a man and a woman. Read together, these two stories underline that in order to live fulfilled lives, we must recognise that we are both spiritual and social creatures. So modern lifestyles that are based on secular values of materialism and consumerism which banish spirituality to the back woods, fly in the face of Genesis. As also does the modern obsession with individualism. Frank Sinatra's classic, 'I did it my way', expresses the personal aspirations of so many today. To be truly human, says Genesis, we need to share our lives with God and with others.

Yet both chapters reflect on the holy and God's place in the world. One way to illustrate this is to investigate the symbolism that is always in the background of chapters 2, 3, to a lesser extent in chapter 1, and echoed in its storyline. While not obvious to a casual reader, there is a great deal of 'sanctuary symbolism' present.[31] The term used for the heavenly 'lights' (*mā'ôr*) created on the fourth day is unusual. Everywhere else in the Pentateuch (the first five books of the Old Testament), it is used for the lights in the sanctuary (e.g. Exodus 25:6; Leviticus 24:2). Similarly, the word often translated 'seasons' (*mô'ēd*, here in the plural), is more accurately rendered '[religious] festivals'. The garden planted by God is in the east (2:8) and entered from the east (3:24), giving it the same orientation as the Old Testament sanctuary (see Numbers 3:38; Ezekiel 8:16), and the restored temple seen in vision by Ezekiel (Ezekiel 44:1).

The Man was placed in the garden 'to work (*'bd*) it and take care of (*šmr*) it' (2:15). These same verbs are used in combination elsewhere to describe the duties of priests in the sanctuary (Numbers 3:7, 8; 8:26; 18:7). One of the rivers that arises in Eden is the Gihon (2:13). Elsewhere in the Bible this is unknown as a river. However, due south of the temple area in Jerusalem is a spring of water, also known as the Gihon, the site of Solomon's coronation (1 Kings 1:38, 39), and the source for Hezekiah's famous aqueduct that provided water for Jerusalem (2 Chronicles 32:30). Just as rivers flowed out of Eden and watered the whole earth, so in prophetic vision waters flowed from the temple and brought fertility to desert places, nourishing miraculous trees (Ezekiel 47:1-12, especially v. 12 cf Gen. 2:9b-10a). [32]

Finally, after the tragedy of the next chapter, God placed cherubim at the entrance to the garden (3:24). Cherubim were prominent in the design of the Israelite sanctuary (e.g. Exodus 25:19), Solomon's temple (e.g. 1 Kings 6:24-27), and Ezekiel's vision of God's glory in the restored temple (e.g. Ezekiel 9:3). Cherubim are mentioned almost one hundred times in the Old Testament, and Genesis 3:24 is one of only two references that do not explicitly connect them to the sanctuary. Significantly, the other reference that does not is Ezekiel 28:13-14, where in poetic imagery the king of Tyre is addressed as having been, *'in Eden, the garden of God'*; every precious stone adorned you: ruby, topaz and emerald, chrysolite, onyx and jasper, sapphire, turquoise and beryl. Your settings and mountings were made of gold; on the day you were created they were prepared. You were anointed as a *guardian cherub*, for so I ordained you. You were on the *holy mount* of God.' It is surely significant that Ezekiel not only links 'Eden' with 'cherub', but also that all of the jewels and gold mentioned were also present in the sanctuary, on the vestments and breastplates of the high priest (Exodus 28:15-29). What is more, the term 'holy mount' is a common reference to Mount Zion, on which the Jerusalem temple stood (e.g. Psalms 48 and 87, etc.). In conclusion, we should not miss that 'rest is the principal function of a temple, and a temple is always where deity finds rest'.[33] And that is precisely what God does on the seventh day.

What is the significance of these points of contact? The first account of creation concluded with *holy time* on the seventh day. The second account of creation in particular, utilises the symbolism of the sanctuary, that is, *holy space*. God later said to Moses, 'have them make a sanctuary for me, and I will dwell among them' (Exodus 25:8). The sanctuary represents the presence of God. So, far from being a mundane chronicle of the origins of time and space, these opening chapters of Genesis lay before us the importance of holy time and holy space. In the beginning, Sabbath and Sanctuary underline God's presence in time and space. The time in which we live, and the space in which we move, everything that defines what we are and what we do, is played out in the presence of God. These are not simple stories for naive readers, but narratives that delve into the profound mysteries of the meaning of life. They put before us what it means to be human, who God is and how we should live in his world.

[25] The sequence 'heaven(s) and (the) earth', is used at least thirty times in the Old Testament. There are only three examples of the reverse, 'earth and (the) heaven(s)', in Gen 2:4; Ps 148:13; Ezek 8:3.

[26] For example, Romans 12:6-8; 1 Corinthians 12:1-31.

[27] The Infinitive absolute followed by some form of the Imperfect of the same verb. Further examples of this construction are found in Genesis 18:10; 22:17; 1 Samuel 9:6, etc.

[28] For other examples see Gen. 20:7; 1 Sam. 14:44; 22:16; 1 Kings 2:37, etc.

[29] NIV translates 2:19 as, 'Now the Lord God *had* formed out of the ground all the beasts of the field and all the birds of the air.' This requires that the creatures had been formed prior to this. However, the sequence of events argues against this: a) God announces that he *will* make a helper for the Man (2:18); b) he then proceeds to create the animals (2:19); but c) among them was found no helper for the Man (2:20). As far as I am aware, NIV is the only modern English version to render 2:19 as a pluperfect.

[30] See *HALOT*. Also, for example, New Revised Standard Version; New Jerusalem Bible.

[31] For more detail on some of the points mentioned here see, for example, G. J. Wenham, 'Sanctuary Symbolism in the Garden of Eden Story', in *Proceedings of the World Congress of Jewish Studies 9* (1986), pp. 19-25.

[32] It has also been suggested, on the basis of archaeological evidence, that the seven-branched candlestick in the temple was a stylised tree, with a central stem and branches – that is, the tree of life, also in the garden of Eden. See Wenham, 'Sanctuary Symbolism', pp. 19-25.

[33] Walton, 'Creation', p. 165.

CHAPTER FOUR
The Serpent's Seduction
Genesis 3

The division between chapters 1 and 2 came at an unfortunate place, making a break between the sixth and seventh days of creation. In the same way, we should not be misled by the break between chapters 2 and 3. These two chapters are actually one extended story rather than two individual ones. It is important to keep the two chapters together in our minds as we read them.

So far in Genesis we have met three major characters: God, the Man and the Woman. Here we meet a fourth – the Serpent. He turns out to be a mysterious personality, yet absolutely vital for understanding how the story takes a dramatic turn. Some have referred to him as the first theologian in the Bible. That is, he does not speak *to* God or *with* God, he merely speaks *about* God – theologians beware!

But who exactly is he? Why does he do what he does? We are told that he 'was more crafty than any of the wild animals the Lord God had made' (3:1). So, he is part of God's creation. But since God has created everything – 'the heavens and the earth' – that adds little to our understanding.

Not surprisingly, there have been several suggestions as to his identity. The natural Christian solution is to see him as Satan in disguise, or at least a representative of the evil one. That is understandable when we read some New Testament texts. For example, John writes of 'that ancient serpent called the devil, or Satan, who leads the whole world astray' (Revelation 12:9), and of 'that ancient serpent, who is the devil, or Satan' (Revelation 20:2). And Paul probably also has the Serpent in mind when he echoes Gen. 3:15, 'The God of peace will soon crush Satan under your feet' (Romans 16:20). These texts certainly help the Christian's understanding, but they are all from the New Testament. Genesis makes no explicit mention of Satan, a fact that often takes readers by surprise. What is even more surprising, perhaps, is that Satan is mentioned in only three passages in the whole Old Testament (1 Chronicles 21:1; Job 1, 2; Zechariah 3:1, 2). This does not mean that we should not see Satan somewhere in this text, but the fact that Genesis does not mention him suggests that there is something more important than seeing that.

So who exactly is the Serpent? There are those who take him to be merely another wild animal and who see the story as an explanation of why humans are scared of snakes. But in an account dealing with extremely significant issues of creation and human destiny, it seems odd to deal with this relatively marginal point. For others, the Serpent exists only in the minds of the characters. So, when the 'Serpent' speaks to Eve, it is really she herself, debating within her own mind the pros and cons of disobeying God.

As attractive as this might be for some modern readers, the story certainly seems to present the Serpent as separate from the Woman. The fact that God addresses both of them individually (3:14-16), also argues against this suggestion.[34]

However, the fact that Genesis does not reveal the identity of the Serpent is significant in itself. We are not told why he tempts the Man and Woman nor how he knows what God has said to them. God asks the Man and Woman to explain their actions, but not the Serpent. We have not met him before and after his deed here he leaves, never to be seen again. This lack of information makes him mysterious – and this is precisely the point Genesis wants to make. The origins of sin can never be fully understood. So the story conceals more than it reveals on this topic. It tells us enough for us to know *what* happened, but not enough for us fully to understand *why*. There are limits to what we can understand, and there are limits to what has been revealed. As Scripture reminds us elsewhere, 'The secret things belong to the Lord our God, but the things revealed belong to us and to our children for ever' (Deuteronomy 29:29).

This part of the story begins with a play on words, demonstrating that chapters 2 and 3 form one continuous story. Chapter 2 concluded by saying that the human pair were 'naked' ('arôm, 2:25). Chapter 3 begins by telling us that the Serpent was 'crafty' ('arûm, 3:1). This ominous 'arôm/'arûm wordplay advertises that the human nakedness, their openness, innocence and lack of shame in their personal relationship, is now under threat from the Serpent.

The craftiness of the Serpent is shown in his ability to lie. He begins with a deliberate exaggeration, 'Did God really say, "You must not eat from any tree in the garden"?' (3:1b). His tone of voice is barely disguised amazement at the stupidity of such a divine command. But he is also subtle, not contradicting God outright at this stage, but asking a question in such a way that the only reasonable response must surely be to agree with him.

The Woman, however, is eager to disagree with him and to defend God against the insinuation that he is unreasonable. But is she too eager? She responds that the Serpent is wrong. God has prohibited them from eating fruit from only *one* tree in the garden. In fact, she says, God commanded that they 'must not touch it' (3:3). But had he? Not according to Genesis 2:16-17, where God gave the original command, at a time before the Woman was created. She seems to be slightly over-zealous in her defence of God.

So the Serpent, master strategist that he is, moves from innuendo to direct opposition of God, forcing her to make a choice between himself and God. When God had originally spoken to the Man, the consequences of disobedience were clear, literally, 'dying you shall die' (2:17). The Serpent now raises the stakes by saying, literally, '*not* dying you shall die' (3:4). Having drawn the Woman into his net, he now shows how cunning he is. He provides no elaborate argument against God, but simply a flat contradiction. One of the basic rules of being a successful liar is to keep it simple. Once we embellish our deceit with many details and complicated denials we lower our chance of success by providing our intended victims with potential ammunition to use against us.

After his simple denial of God's prediction, the Serpent gives his version of God's true motivation for denying the Woman access to the tree. It is clear, he alleges, that 'God knows that when you eat of it your eyes will be opened, and you will be like God, knowing good and evil' (3:5). When God had forbidden access to the tree, it is true that he provided no reason, inviting them to trust him. The Serpent now plays on this. Will the Woman trust God or believe him? But what is he asking her to believe? In order to understand the developments in this story we must have a clear view of what exactly the Serpent's temptation was.

There are three main elements: a) their eyes will be opened; b) they will become like God; c) they will know good and evil. Let us begin with the second element, becoming like God.

At first sight, this is a strange temptation, for they are already like God. They were created in the image of God, after his likeness (1:26-27). But of course, they were not created like God in every respect. Here the temptation is to close the gap, appealing to a possible sense of injustice. What does God have that they do not have? He has the third element in the temptation, a knowledge of good and evil. This they will have, suggests the Serpent, if they will only trust him rather than God. They will receive not only insight, (having their 'eyes opened'), but divine power to know good and evil.

'The knowledge of good and evil' is mentioned four times in chapters 2 and 3 (2:9, 17; 3:5, 22). However, why would it be a temptation to possess it? In order to understand the most likely intention of the Serpent, we need to examine two elements in particular.

First, he said that they would 'know' (yd') good and evil. This Hebrew verb is used to convey the idea of intellectual knowledge, as when Abraham said to his wife Sarah, 'I know (yd') what a beautiful woman you are' (Genesis 12:11). But it has broader connotations. It is one of the verbs commonly used to describe sexual relations. For example, in the next chapter we read literally, 'Now Adam knew (yd') Eve his wife, and she conceived and bore Cain' (4:1, NKJV). Clearly, the Woman's conception and giving birth was the result of more than Adam's intellectual knowledge. The prophets talk of 'knowing' or having 'knowledge of' God. For example, ' "He defended the cause of the poor and needy, and so all went well. Is that not what it means to know me?" declares the Lord' (Jeremiah 22:16). To know God is to act out the consequences of simple intellectual knowledge. Clearly, the verb can carry the meaning of intimate understanding, or experience of.

The second element to consider is 'good and evil'. This is an example of a Hebrew idiom (technically known as *merismus*). When the Hebrews wanted to make an all-encompassing statement, they would sometimes express it by putting together two elements from two opposite extremes. For example, 'During Solomon's lifetime Judah and Israel, from *Dan* to *Beersheba*, lived in safety' (1 Kings 4:25). Dan was a town in the extreme north of Israel, and Beersheba was in the far south. Placed side by side they convey the idea of the whole country of Israel. An earlier example of this idiom is found in Genesis 1:1, where 'heaven and earth' is used to convey 'everything'.

The terms 'good and evil' are also extreme opposites, and are used in the same way. For example, 'Absalom never said a word to Amnon, either *good* or *bad*' (2 Samuel 13:22). Clearly, this means that Absalom said *nothing* to Amnon. When the inhabitants of Jerusalem say, 'The Lord will not do *good*, nor will he do *evil*' (Zephaniah 1:12, NKJV), they are accusing him of doing *nothing*. When the two terms are used together they mean more than the sum of their parts. In just the same way, in English we might say, 'It's raining cats and dogs'. We would be misled if we thought the meaning of this English idiom could be worked out by analysing, separately, the meaning of 'cats' and 'dogs'.

So, when the Serpent told the Woman that she and her husband would be able 'to know good and evil', he meant that they would be able *to experience everything*. And in that sense they would 'become like God'. For no one places restrictions on God. He acts as he wishes. So the temptation is to be as free as God is. If the Serpent were telling the truth, this would be the greatest of all temptations.

How does the Woman respond this time? Previously she had

seen the tree of the knowledge of good and evil as completely off-limits. Now she reconsiders, and looks at it through the eyes of the Serpent. She makes three observations (3:6). First, it 'was good for food'; it appealed at a purely practical level. Secondly, it was 'pleasing to the eye'; it appealed to her aesthetic appreciation of what was beautiful. Thirdly, and most importantly, it was 'desirable for gaining wisdom'; that is, she now agrees with the Serpent that the tree is not a threat but an opportunity to 'know good and evil'.

However, wasn't it unfair of God to make this crucial tree so attractive? It is important to see that it is no more attractive than any other tree in the garden. When God had planted the garden, he 'made all kinds of trees grow out of the ground – trees that were pleasing to the eye and good for food' (2:9). So, *all* the trees in the garden are 'pleasing to the eye and good for food'. From the Woman's point of view, what distinguishes this one tree from all the rest is that it has the power 'for gaining wisdom'. She cannot know that, simply by looking at it, but only by believing the Serpent rather than God. This is an ominous turn of events. Just how ominous is underlined when we consider that humans were supposed to have dominion over the animals. But the first animal they meet, the Serpent, now has dominion over them.

So, 'she took some and ate it. She also gave some to her husband, who was with her, and he ate it' (3:6). Amazingly the Man follows his wife's example without any protest. The result is that 'the eyes of both of them were opened' (3:7) – exactly as the Serpent had promised. Well, not exactly. For he had promised that once their eyes were opened they '*would be like God*'; but here, their eyes were opened 'and *they realised that they were naked*'. What a disappointment! The Serpent had been economical with the truth. Rather than starting a new life of complete freedom, with all restrictions removed, the reverse is actually the case, as we shall soon see. It also becomes apparent that their nakedness is not simply physical but also personal and spiritual.

Notice how the incidental details build up a picture of their dilemma. Both of them 'heard the sound of the Lord God as he was walking in the garden in the cool of the day, and they hid from the Lord God among the trees of the garden' (3:8). What they heard in the garden could equally well be translated as 'the voice of the Lord God' (e.g. KJV). They had heard God's voice before, of course. For example, when he had blessed them and given them food (1:28, 29), forbidden fruit from the tree of the knowledge of good and evil (2:16, 17), and announced that he would provide a partner for the Man (2:18). The voice of God was familiar; but the human reaction this time was not. They hid from God. That simple statement indicates the scale of the catastrophe. Previously the Lord God had formed the Man from the dust of the ground, and built up the Man's rib into a woman. He had been involved with them both creatively and intimately. But now they both hide from him. Instead of intimacy, there is alienation. And the scale of the alienation is revealed when the Man says, 'I was afraid because I was naked; so I hid' (3:10). Note that his nakedness does not make him embarrassed, but afraid. Fear marks the absence of understanding and trust.

The depth of the problem is revealed in God's questions. He did not simply ask the Man a question, but he 'called to the man'. That is, he stands at a distance and calls. This is no intimate chat, but communication by use of a megaphone.

The question is, 'Where are you?' (3:9). Doesn't God know where the Man is? Of course he does.[35] But does *the Man* know where he is? Well, he obviously knows that he's hiding among the trees. But it's a deeper question than that. And so is the question he asks of the Woman, 'What is this you have done?' (3:13).

Each of those questions can receive a simple answer, which the Man and Woman actually provide. These questions, however, do not simply request information. They invite the Man and Woman to ponder their position and actions. And they challenge us as readers to do the same. 'Where are *you*?', the text asks of us individually. In our relationship with God, exactly where are we? Hiding, like the Man?

The second question to the Woman, 'What is this *you* have done?', is a sharp reminder of our individual moral responsibility. Just how important these questions are in chapter 3 will become even clearer when we turn to chapter 4.

With a few quick strokes of the pen, the story shows how trusting the Serpent rather than God shatters their relationships, not only that between themselves, but also that between themselves and God. We saw how the first creation account emphasised our relationship with God (1:26; 2:7), while the second, in addition to that, underlined our relationships with one another (2:23-25). Here, both of these relationships change, never to be the same again. This is summed up by the Man's response to God's question, 'The woman you put here with me – she gave me some fruit from the tree, and I ate it' (3:12). At one level this is factually correct, but one can hear the tone of accusation in his words. Not content with blaming his wife, he also blames God. The selfish motivation for believing the Serpent's lie is now made clear. The Man and Woman might have sinned together, but it did not keep them together, because the essence of sin is selfishness.

The fact that God interrogates the human couple is significant. They are given the opportunity to explain themselves because we are responsible for our actions. Despite the tendency of our time to find excuses in the deficiencies of our environment or upbringing, and even allowing for mitigating circumstances, we are generally responsible for what we do. The buck stops with us.[36] Yet the Man blamed the Woman and God. The Woman blamed the Serpent. And the Serpent blamed no one because he wasn't asked. Given the opportunity he would surely have blamed someone else as well. Who might it have been?

The first creation account was peppered with blessings (1:22, 28; 2:3). Just how radically matters have turned around is demonstrated by the curses at the end of chapter 3. In particular, the curses affect the original threefold blessings found in Genesis 1:28. The first, addressed to the Serpent, concerns dominion over the animals, ' "Cursed are you above all the livestock and all the wild animals! . . . I will put enmity between you and the woman, and between your offspring and hers; he will crush your head, and you will strike his heel" ' (3:14-15).

Note that the Serpent was first introduced as being 'crafty'
('arûm); he departs having been cursed ('arûr). Originally,
humans were to have dominion, but now there will be outright
antagonism – at least with part of the animal creation. The
second curse, on the Woman, complicates the command to be
fruitful and multiply, ' "I will greatly increase your pains in
childbearing; with pain you will give birth to children. Your desire
will be for your husband, and he will rule over you" ' (3:16). If
women experience painful childbirth, then they might well have
fewer children. But sexual desire will ensure that they continue
to give birth. What is more, the curse also transforms the
equality between the sexes, seen up to now, into male
domination.

Finally, the curse on the Man echoes the previous command
that humans should 'subdue the earth'. ' "Cursed is the ground
because of you; . . . It will produce thorns and thistles for you,
. . . you [will] return to the ground, since from it you were taken;
for dust you are and to dust you will return." ' (3:17-19). The
earth will become a much less hospitable place for the Man. If
the Man returns to the dust of the earth, then it looks as if the
earth will subdue him rather than vice-versa.

Two of the curses in particular, those on the Serpent and the
Woman, have attracted attention. The curse on the Serpent is
sometimes called the *protevangelium*, or 'first gospel'. It
announces the fate of the Serpent, the agent who seduced
humanity to sin. We must be careful not to over-interpret it, for
like many other aspects of this chapter, it is enigmatic. It does
not set out clearly an image of Jesus Christ dying for the sins of
the world on Calvary. But, by showing the future fate of the
Serpent it announces ultimate victory over the forces opposed
to God. At the time when God first has to deal with the dilemma
of sin, it is hinted that one day it will be overcome (see e.g.
Romans 16:20; Revelation 20:2).

In order to understand the curse on the Woman, we must
consider the curse on the Man. Put simply, the Man was formed
from the ground, and his curse is to be dominated by it. The
Woman was formed from the Man, and her curse is to be
dominated by him. The principle is that the Man and the

Woman will both be mastered by their origins. Hebrew wordplay is used to show their close connection. The Man (*'adam*), was formed from the ground (*'ᵃdāmâ*) (2:7); the Woman (*iššâ*) came from the Man (*îš*) (2:23).

The curse on the Woman is prominent in some debates about the 'biblical' view of marriage and the ordination of women. But when reading this passage we need to weigh its details and context. It is true that just as the sun and moon were appointed 'to govern (*māšal*) the day and the night' (1:18), so the Woman is told, 'your husband . . . will rule (*māšal*) over you' (3:16). But the context of each statement is very different. When God gave the sun and moon power to govern the day and night, 'God saw that it was good' (1:18). It conformed to his will. But the curse on the Woman is clearly not what God originally wanted.

Wherever we see men dominating women, we see the effects of sin. That needs to be born in mind when looking at the curse on the Man. There, the Man is to be dominated by the ground. Wherever we see the frustrations and failures of agriculture – drought, plague, weed infestation, disease, etc. – we also see the effects of sin. If the curses are taken to *prescribe* what must be, then not only should women submit to male domination, but men should use neither chemical nor mechanical help in working the ground.

But if these curses *describe* the effect of sin, then we are free to resist the effects of sin in this world.[37] That is to say, we oppose God no more by working for women's equality with men than we do by using fertiliser and weedkiller in our garden.

Despite the negative tone of much of this chapter, there is at least something positive at its conclusion. God had told them that if they ate from the forbidden tree, they would definitely die. But they don't. Now, of course, we could say that something did die the day they disobeyed – perhaps their relationship with God, or with each other. That would be true, but that was not God's main meaning when he uttered those words, as we saw previously. We should not be afraid of simply accepting that what God said would happen did not happen. The objection might be, 'Then you can't trust God. He says one thing and does another.' The rest of Scripture makes it clear that we can trust God. And we can trust him not to give us what we truly deserve. We call this 'grace'. God 'changes his mind'. We'll discuss this more when we look at the story of the flood. But God is not capricious. When he changes his mind it is almost without fail to our advantage. We benefit from it, and do not suffer as a consequence.

That does not mean that there is no cursing or punishment in this story, however. But they are not the whole story. That balance is summed up by God when he removes the clothes of fig leaves that they have used to cover their nakedness, and replaces them with animal skins (3:21). On the one hand it is an act of grace, giving them something better and more durable than they had. But it also underlines that their alienation from God and from each other is permanent. Hard-wearing garments to cover their nakedness indicate that there is no going back to innocence now.

As we look back on chapters 2 and 3 we see that they form one story, but a story with two distinct halves. In the first half we see the intimacy between the Man, Woman and God. In the second half, the alienation between them. A brief survey of the contrasts will demonstrate the move that has occurred. In chapter 2, God shows his intimate concern by 'forming' the Man and 'breathing' life into him. God provides a partner for the Man, to share her life intimately with him, as 'one flesh'. The way she is created, coming from within the Man himself, underlines how close they are. They are naked before each other, but are neither embarrassed nor self-conscious.

But as we move to chapter 3, that intimacy is ripped apart. They desire independence from God, and prefer to believe the Serpent rather than God. The result is that they become afraid of God. And once their relationship with him has been wrecked, the human pair show that they have lost their mutual respect. For the Man not only blames God but also his wife. The Woman will now be mastered by the Man, and the Man by the earth.

In pondering chapters 2 and 3, thoughtful Christian readers will find a reflection of their own experience. Our relationship with God is never static, but includes spiritual peaks and troughs. The first Man and Woman encounter similar extremes, as they move from intimacy to alienation in their relationship between themselves and God. In our daily experience we too learn that relationships are fragile, frequently devastated by acts of selfishness. On reflection we can see the truth of the basic message of Genesis 2 and 3: a good relationship with God leads to good relationships with each other. Whether we enjoy that experience depends on how responsibly we use the privilege of freedom of choice given to us by God. For good or ill, our choices have consequences.

[34] For more detail, and a bibliography of works discussing the Serpent, see Westermann, *Genesis 1-11*, pp. 237, 8.

[35] Compare the similar 'obvious' question in 4:9.

[36] For a classic Old Testament passage on personal responsibility, see Ezekiel 18.

[37] In any case, the issue of the ordination of women cannot be decided simply by quoting this verse. The New Testament witness must be the most important in that debate.

CHAPTER FIVE
For Whom The Bell Tolls
Genesis 4

A common technique of Hebrew narrators was to tell a story in a certain way, and then to tell another story in such a way that its details would recall and comment on the previous one. We have already seen how the similarities and differences between chapters 1 and 2 achieve this. There is another good example of that tactic here, with numerous parallels between both the words used and the style employed in chapters 3 and 4. Some examples are set out below.[38]

	Chapter 3	*Chapter 4*
Vocabulary		
'Know'	vv. 5, 7, 22	vv. 1, 9
'Work'	v. 23	vv. 2, 12
'Drive out'	v. 24	v. 14
'Ground'	vv. 17, 19, 23	vv. 2, 3, 10-12, 14
	v. 16	v. 7
	'Your desire *(t^ešûqâ)* will be for your husband, and he will rule *(māšal)* over you.'	'[sin] desires *(t^ešûqâ)* to have you, but you must master *(māšal)* it.'

Style/Sequence		
a) Sin committed	v. 6	v. 8
b) Questions from God	v. 9	v. 9
c) Curse on the ground	v. 17	v. 11
d) God's gift to sinners	v. 21 (clothes)	v. 15 (protective mark)
e) Exile eastwards	v. 24	v. 16

These selected points of contact make clear that despite obvious differences, life outside the garden is remarkably similar to life inside the garden. To give one specific example, before they were exiled human beings were given three commands: a) to be fruitful, multiply and fill the earth; b) to subdue the earth; and c) to have dominion over the animals (1:28). Now, outside the garden, they obey all three. The Man and Woman have children (multiplication); Abel keeps sheep (dominion over the animals) and Cain works the ground (subjugation of the earth) (4:1). If only they'd shown the same resolve to obey God's other command, not to eat from the tree of the knowledge of good and evil! But, as we'll soon see, the story takes another turn for the worse.

Many people who read this story have questions concerning Cain's wife (4:17). Where did she come from? We'll deal with her in due course, even though it is quite clear that the story is not much interested in her. By contrast, it is extremely interested in Cain's *brother*. We can see that by the number of times we are reminded of who Abel is. Eve 'gave birth to *his brother* Abel' (4:2). 'Now Cain said to *his brother* Abel, . . . Cain attacked *his brother* Abel . . . "Where is *your brother* Abel?" . . . "Am I *my brother's* keeper?" . . . "*Your brother's* blood cries out to me . . . *your brother's* blood"' (4:8-11). Could it be any clearer? We will not understand this story if we do not see the relationship between these brothers.

But what are we to make of them? Abel is on the scene so fleetingly that he makes only the briefest impression. In fact his name itself is enough to tell us that he won't be around for long. 'Abel' (*hebel*) is a Hebrew word with several meanings, but significantly among these is '(transitory) breath',[39] as in 'Lowborn men are but a breath (*hebel*), the highborn are but a lie; if weighed on a balance, they are nothing; together they are only a breath (*hebel*)' (Psalm 62:9). The focus of this story, then, will be on Cain rather than Abel. Our attention is drawn to him right away by his mother's statement at his birth, ' "With the help of the Lord I have brought forth a man" ' (4:1). However, the meaning of her words is not as straightforward as this translation implies.

There are two problems. The first is the verb translated 'brought forth' (*qānâ*). This is an unusual term to use for childbirth, for it usually means to buy or acquire.[40] Perhaps it is used here merely as a play on words with 'Cain' (*qayin*).

If that part of Eve's statement is puzzling enough, the remainder of what she says is even more so. Translated literally it could be rendered as, 'I have acquired a man the Lord'. But that makes no sense. That is why all English versions have translated it in a similar way to the NIV. Yet some argue that Eve's words mean, 'I have given birth to the Lord' – that is, to the Messiah promised back in Genesis 3:15. However, the word for 'Lord' is Yahweh, or in its more familiar form, Jehovah – the Old Testament name for God. In some English versions it is written in capital letters to distinguish it from 'Lord' (*'ᵃdōnay*), in lower case, referring to a human superior. Are we really to believe that Eve said, in effect, 'I have given birth to Jehovah'! Surely not. That would be not only blasphemous but nonsensical. Not even the virgin Mary said that. And as we've already seen, the promise in Genesis 3:15 gives no precise details, merely promising that the 'seed' of the Woman would crush the Serpent's head. There is no hint that this descendant would be divine in any way. That becomes clearer as we work our way through Scripture, but not at this point.

Nevertheless, let us try to imagine what the birth of Cain, her firstborn, might mean to Eve. She had been promised that her 'seed', i.e. offspring, would crush the head of the Serpent. When she gives birth, therefore, we might well imagine her thinking, 'He's the one! This is my "seed" who will defeat the work of the Serpent.' But to say that her words actually state this is to claim more than the text allows. If Eve believes Cain is the promised one, then what a disappointment he proved to be. Rather than being the foe of the Serpent, he aids and abets him by taking human sin one step further. The Man and Woman had eaten forbidden fruit, and then blamed others. But Cain kills his brother. Eve's tragedy is not so much the pain she experienced in childbirth (3:16), but the ongoing emotional pain her son presumably causes her. In the same way, the curse of sin is not something we experience now and again. It affects all we do and everything we are.

The complication in this story arrives when the two brothers bring an offering to God. It is introduced with no explanation as to its purpose, but it is obviously part of an act of worship by each of them. Cain grows crops, and so he brings them as an offering, while Abel, the shepherd, offers some of his flock.

God's response to each brother, however, is very different, 'The Lord looked with favour on Abel and his offering, but on Cain and his offering he did not look with favour' (4:4, 5). A question asked throughout the ages is why did God accept one offering but reject the other? The reason the question has been discussed so much is that the text doesn't give an explicit answer. Many sincere Christians have assumed that for any offering to be genuine, it must involve the shedding of blood. In fact, doesn't the Epistle to the Hebrews say that? 'The law requires that nearly everything be cleansed with blood, and without the shedding of blood there is no forgiveness' (Hebrews 9:22). So, it is argued, as Cain's offering of vegetables could not possibly contain blood, it was not acceptable to God.

Unfortunately, the issue is not as simple as this. Both brothers brought an 'offering' (*minhâ*) to God (4:3, 4). Basically, this word simply means 'gift'. For example, Jacob sent a gift (*minhâ*) to his brother Esau (Genesis 32:13), while some opponents of Saul brought him no gifts (*minhâ*, 1 Samuel 10:27). More importantly, it is often used in the narrower sense of an offering given in worship to God. And it is quite clear that not all of these offerings required the shedding of blood. In Leviticus 2, for example, a *minhâ* could consist of a grain offering in the form of fine flour mixed with oil and incense (v. 1), unleavened cakes or wafers and oil (v. 4), to which salt must be added (v. 13). If worshippers were too poor to afford a sin offering, which was usually a bull, goat or lamb, then they could offer doves or pigeons instead. But for those too poor to afford even these, an offering of fine flour was acceptable (Leviticus 5:11). There were also 'drink offerings' (*nesek*, e.g. Exodus 30:9, Leviticus 23:13). Such offerings were certainly acceptable to God, so presumably Cain's offering was not rejected simply because it contained no blood.[41] And not every sacrifice in the

Old Testament was designed to forgive sin.[42]

So, what *was* wrong with Cain's offering? The contrast between the two brothers' sacrifices in the story is not so much *what* they brought, but the *quality* of what they brought. Abel brought the 'fat portions from some of the firstborn of his flock' (4:4). He brought the best ('fat portions') of the best ('firstborn'). Cain simply brought, 'some of the fruits of the soil' (4:3), that is, not the best he could, just whatever came to hand. His sacrifice reflected his relationship with God. As the Epistle to the Hebrews says, 'By faith Abel offered God a better sacrifice than Cain did' (Hebrews 11:4). In other words, it was his attitude to God that made the difference, not a technical point about the content of his sacrifice. By faith, Cain could have presented an offering as acceptable as Abel's. Not by sacrificing one of Abel's lambs, but by giving the best he could.

So the story of Cain and Abel, often remembered as a murder story, invites us to ponder the quality of our relationship with God. At creation, God saw all that he had made and, 'it was very good' (1:31). That is what he gave to us, as his representatives in creation. This story reminds us that what we give to God in return, also needs to be the best we can give. Gifts are devalued in our society. For example, very few of us *give* Christmas presents. We *exchange* them. A true gift is one that is given with no thought of receiving anything in return. By faith, Abel offered a better sacrifice than Cain did, because he saw that only his best was good enough for God.

Yet all was not lost simply because Cain's sacrifice was inadequate. God is understanding and offers Cain advice. God encourages him to change his attitude and if he does so, he will be accepted. God's question, 'If you do what is right, will you not be accepted?' (4:7), has an obvious answer – of course he will be. But he needs to master his sinful desires, which are ready to pounce and overcome him. Quite clearly, God is trying to mend the relationship between the two of them. But he will not force the issue. Cain needs to face up to the problem and change his attitudes. How this story will end depends on whether Cain chooses to accept or reject God's advice.

We are not told how soon after this the next stage in the

story takes place. Nor are we told that Cain murders Abel because God rejected his offering but accepted Abel's. Nor, despite what English versions tell us, do we know what Cain said to Abel. Cain's words, 'Let's go out to the field' (4:8), are entirely lacking in the Hebrew text. They are found only in some ancient versions that tried to make sense of the omission. We've already met similar omissions in the preceding stories. Too many readers of these Genesis stories have been too eager to fill in the gaps. But we must be extremely careful not to fill them in and then treat the fillings as if they are part of Scripture. Many people who take the time to read the Bible carefully, suddenly discover that many things they knew were there are not there at all. Simply reading this story, we cannot be certain when Cain spoke to his brother, what he said to him, nor why he killed him. It isn't important to know any of those things. The less we know, the more irrational Cain's sin becomes. The one thing that is necessary for us to know is that Cain has not mastered his sinful desires (4:7). What the story is really interested in is the effect of sin on Cain.

Chapter 3 showed us how sin fractured the relationships that the Man and Woman had with God and themselves. Cain now accelerates that move towards moral and spiritual chaos.

In chapter 3 the Serpent had to seduce the humans into doing the wrong thing. But here, God himself can not even persuade Cain to do the right thing. How far matters have developed can be seen by investigating God's questions.

Two stand out.

God's question to Adam, 'Where are *you*?' (3:9) was difficult enough. But Cain is asked to ponder more pointedly, 'Where is *your brother*?' (4:9a). At least Adam answered God's question, even though he accused God. But Cain responds with a simple lie, 'I don't know'. He then questions God, 'Am I my brother's keeper?' In this he is being sarcastic, because 'keeper' (*šōmer*) is the Hebrew for 'shepherd' – Abel's occupation. Once again, just as in chapter 3, these questions are directed not only to the characters, but also to us. If we cannot answer 'Where are you?', or 'Where is your brother?', then we are not living as God intended. And how would we respond to Cain's question, 'Am I my brother's keeper?' Do we, or do we not, have responsibilities toward our fellow human beings? If Cain *had* been his brother's keeper, then Abel would not have been murdered.

Just as his evasion of God's question is more obvious than Adam's, the nature of his sin is more serious. As a consequence, his curse is more severe. In the garden the Man was told, 'Cursed is the ground because of you' (3:17), but Cain will be, 'driven from the ground' (4:11). Here, it is not the ground, but Cain, that is cursed. The connection between Man ('*ādām*) and the ground ('*dāmâ*), once so intimate, is becoming increasingly distant. In the beginning God brought physical order out of physical chaos. But beginning in Eden, and continuing with Cain, the world is moving increasingly from moral order to moral chaos.

The human dilemma is summed up by Cain's response to his punishment. The questioning of the Man and Woman in the garden reminded them that they were morally responsible creatures. But there is no sense of moral responsibility in Cain's words. He offers no confession, not even a request for forgiveness. The only thing he acknowledges is his own dire state, 'My punishment is more than I can bear' (4:13). He expresses fear that he, a murderer, should be murdered in turn (4:14). At no point does he express any concern for his dead brother. This should not surprise us, after seeing how selfishness tore apart human relationships in the garden. Cain takes the possibilities of selfishness one step further.

Despite all this, God acts on Cain's behalf. Just as God showed grace to the couple he expelled from Eden, providing them with clothing, so to Cain he gives a mark. We will seriously misinterpret this story if we see the mark as part of the curse, as many over the centuries have done. Ideas about his mark have ranged from the whimsical (a pathetic expression on his face), to the racist (the black skin of the African that set him apart for slavery). We do not know what the mark was, but whatever it was, it *protected* Cain. It was a gift of God's grace. Just as the Man and Woman did not die on the day they disobeyed, so Cain's mark will protect him from vengeance.

Despite the fact that human beings are sinners, God is a God of grace. That much is abundantly clear.

The human story had started in Eden. It now moves on to the land of Nod (4:16). A play on words explains the significance of this place. God had told Cain that he would be 'a restless wanderer (*nod*) on the earth' (4:12). Cain himself acknowledges this by repeating God's sentence verbatim (4:14). So, we are told, 'Cain went out from the Lord's presence and lived in the land of *Nod*, east of Eden' (4:16). The 'land of Nod' is not so much a spot on the map. Rather, it describes the state of Cain, in his restless and aimless moral chaos, not acknowledging his responsibility towards either his brother or God. Yet, despite this, his mark is a constant reminder to him of God's grace.

The story of Cain and Abel may be simple, but nevertheless raises important issues for the Christian reader. God's rejection of Cain's sacrifice underlines the importance of worship. God created us not only with the capacity to worship, but with the *need* to worship. If we do not worship him, we run the risk of worshipping our own desires and lusts. In recent years a great deal of innovation has taken place in public worship. The story of Cain suggests that whether our worship is personal or public, traditional or contemporary, God expects us to give him our very best.

We saw in chapter 2 how we were created as social beings, designed to share our lives with others. Unlike modern western society, Genesis does not glorify individualism. With the rest of Scripture it affirms that our lives are fulfilled through co-operative and generous relationships with God and other people. Cain demonstrates the tragic results that occur when individualism and self-centredness replace those ideals. He also illustrates why we were not created with absolute freedom to do whatever we wish, with no repercussions. It is in this light that we should view God's curse on Cain. It announces that we are morally responsible for our actions, that what we do, whether good or evil, has consequences. Cain's response, 'My punishment is more than I can bear' (4:13), – that is, 'It's not fair!' – simply confirms how self-centred he is. He is the typical human being who believes that others should treat him according to God's principles, but those same principles do not apply to himself.

Despite everything, God does not reject Cain. He punishes him, but also shows him the way forward. God runs the risk of being judged inconsistent because he is a God of grace. God's care and concern for Cain, despite his sin, should encourage anyone who falls short of God's ideal.

Genesis 4:17-26

To a modern western reader, the next section begins in an unpromising way. It gives brief mention of what Cain did next and then launches into a genealogical list of his descendants. We are tempted to skip over this seemingly boring catalogue, and move on to more interesting matters. But that would be a mistake. The genealogies are an essential part of the book. However, we need to understand why they are there and how they operate, if we are to appreciate just how interesting they are. We will investigate the genealogy of 4:17-26, and all of the other genealogies in the primaeval history, in the next chapter.

First, let us quickly note that Cain married a wife (4:17). Where did she come from? She could have been his sister. But since the text gives no indication of when he married her, before or long after he killed Abel, she could have been some other relative. Marriage to close relatives was practised in the ancient world. Elsewhere in Genesis Nahor married his brother Haran's daughter (11:29), and Abraham claims Sarah is his half-sister (20:12).

But more important than the wife he married was the 'city' he built. Let us not be hoodwinked into thinking that this was some grand enterprise. A city, as we think of it, needs many people to populate it. Yet in this story there could hardly have been enough to make an encampment.[43] Perhaps the word 'city' is chosen carefully to remind us that Cain has been doomed to be a 'restless wanderer', and his attempt at establishing a settled 'city' shows that he is as defiant in exile as he was when talking to God after his brother's murder.

However, the focus of this section is not on Cain but on Lamech, the individual whose family concludes this list. The other generations are hurriedly listed in two verses, but Lamech takes up six verses with full family details and a full-blown speech. We should, perhaps, be more interested in Lamech's two wives than in Cain's one wife. The ideal for marriage in the beginning seems clearly to have been monogamy (see 2:24). Lamech's bigamy might be one more indication that God's intention for humanity is unravelling even more.[44] This is all the more likely when we see how Lamech compares himself to Cain. 'I have killed a man for wounding me, a young man for injuring me. If Cain is avenged seven times, then Lamech seventy-seven times' (4:23-24). We have already been shocked by the brutality and immorality of Cain. But compared to Lamech, Cain is insignificant. Humanity seems to be heading towards total depravity. If Cain moved the world one step further away from God's moral order towards moral chaos, then Lamech accelerates the lurch towards anarchy. The genealogical list of 4:17-24 underlines the problem by beginning with one murderer, Cain, and concluding with another, Lamech. How God will deal with this dilemma is picked up in chapter 6.

The passage concludes on a more positive note with Eve's words announcing the birth of Seth (4:25). A moment's reflection reveals that his birth here is chronologically out of place. The next chapter shows that Adam was 130 years old when Seth was born. So Seth was born many years before Lamech, who is six generations beyond Adam. Why not introduce Seth before? By not mentioning him until now, Eve's speech includes all three of her sons in one breath (4:25). Abel was killed and Cain is an exiled murderer. Seth injects some hope into the story. At the birth of Cain we had speculated that Eve may have thought that he was the 'seed' (*zera'*), promised in 3:15, the one who would defeat the Serpent. We might be closer to the mark in believing that she thought Seth was the one. For her words are literally, 'God has granted me another *seed* (*zera'*)' This is the first use of the word since God's original promise, and suggests that for Eve God's promise still lives. Seth's son Enosh begins a new line of descent that strikes off in another direction. 'At that time men began to call on the name of the Lord' (4:26). This can hardly mean that people now started to use 'Yahweh' ('Lord') when they addressed God, because Eve had called him that at the birth of Cain. Perhaps it refers to formal public worship. (Though Cain and Abel had brought personal offerings to God before, of course.) Whatever it means, it indicates a positive shift away from the murderous act of Cain and the chilling selfishness of Lamech. There is some hope, therefore, in the line of Seth.

[38] For more details see G.J. Wenham, *Genesis 1-15* (Word Biblical Commentary 1; Waco, TX: Word Books, 1987), p. 99.

[39] *HALOT.*

[40] *HALOT.*

[41] For a full discussion of this issue, see R. Youngblood, *The Genesis Debate: Persistent Questions About Creation and the Flood* (Grand Rapids: Baker Book House, 1990), pp. 130-47.

[42] For example, Leviticus 3 which sets out legislation for 'fellowship offerings' does not mention sin at all. By contrast 'sin' is mentioned repeatedly in Leviticus 4 which contains legislation for 'sin offerings.'

[43] The word itself (*'îr*), simply describes a 'permanent settlement without any reference to its size or importance' (HALOT.)

[44] There are of course examples of men with more than one wife in the rest of Scripture (e.g. Jacob, David, Solomon). But these are the exception rather than the rule, and it would be difficult to claim that their stories advocate the practice.

CHAPTER SIX
This, Too, Tells a Story
Genesis 5

At first sight Genesis 5 appears to be, frankly, tedious. And it must be admitted that to the uninitiated the catalogue of names and ages adds nothing to our understanding of God's ways in the world. But the Genesis genealogies are actually just as interesting as the narratives, once we take the time to investigate them. Once we know the nature of these genealogies we will be better able to understand their function in the book and what they contribute to its message.

It has often been assumed, especially by those who have a conservative view of Scripture, that the primary purpose of the genealogies is to provide us with chronological information that can be used for historical purposes. On this view, by looking at the life-spans in the Genesis genealogies, we can calculate the age of life on earth, the date of the Flood and so on. There are more than enough books that deal with these historical and scientific issues, so I will not attempt to duplicate what they say. What is worth noting briefly, however, is that using the genealogies to calculate the date of significant events is not as easy as it might first seem. Genesis has been preserved in three traditions: the Masoretic Text (the standard Hebrew text); the Samaritan Pentateuch (copied separately by the Samaritans) and the Septuagint (the Greek translation). They are not in absolute agreement about the ages of those mentioned in the genealogy of Genesis 5, as the following chart indicates. Note that X = the father's age when the first child was born; Y = the remaining years of the father's life; X+Y = the father's age at death.[45]

	Masoretic Text [MT]			Samaritan Pentateuch [SP]		
	X	Y	X+Y	X	Y	X+Y
Adam	130	800	930	130	800	930
Seth	105	807	912	105	807	912
Enosh	90	815	905	90	815	905
Kenan	70	840	910	70	840	910
Mahalalel	65	830	895	65	830	895
Jared	162	800	962	62	785	847
Enoch	65	300	365	65	300	365
Methuselah	187	782	969	67	653	720
Lamech	182	595	777	53	600	653
Noah	500	–	–	500	–	–
Till Flood	100	–	–	100	–	–
Date Flood	1656	–	–	1307	–	–

The differences between the individual ages, especially those of the father when his first son was born, result in very different dates for the Flood, expressed as years since creation. These chronological issues in the genealogies are what usually preoccupy readers. However, the genealogies are not merely concerned with chronology, but also with theology. They reveal as much about God as the stories do.

The Hebrew word for 'genealogy' or 'generations' is *tôlᵉdôt*.[46] It is used throughout Genesis as a title for the lists of people descended from a common ancestor. The one exception to this is the first example in the book. Genesis 2:4a is the last line of the creation account that started in 1:1, and it summarises creation week as being, 'the genealogy (*tôlᵉdôt*) of the heavens and the earth when they were created'.[47] So, the creation account is a genealogy, not of human beings but of the world. It describes how God made the 'heavens and the earth' in six days and rested on the seventh. The seventh day is

Septuagint [LXX]			Date of Death After Creation			
X	Y	X+Y	MT	SP	LXX	
230	700	930	930	930	930	Adam
205	707	912	1042	1042	1142	Seth
190	715	905	1140	1140	1340	Enosh
170	740	910	1235	1235	1535	Kenan
165	730	895	1290	1290	1690	Mahalalel
162	800	962	1422	1307	1922	Jared
165	200	365	987	887	1487	Enoch
167	802	969	1656	1307	2256	Methuselah
188	565	753	1651	1307	2207	Lamech
500	–	–	–	–	–	Noah
100	–	–	–	–	–	*Till Flood*
2242	–	–	–	–	–	*Date Flood*

distinguished from the other six in several ways: God rested on it and blessed and sanctified it. It contains none of the repeated elements found on all of the other days (see comments on ch. 1). So, to restate the obvious but critical point, this genealogy (tôl°dôt) of Gen 1:1-2:4a has six main elements concluded by a seventh which is distinguished from all of the others.

The next genealogical list is 4:17-24 (although the term tôl°dôt is not used). Adam is not mentioned by name, but the list takes the reader down to Lamech, the seventh generation from Adam:

1. (Adam)
2. Cain
3. Enoch
4. Irad
5. Mehujael
6. Methushael
7. Lamech

So just as the first (creation) genealogy, this one also ends with the seventh element, Lamech. And just as with the seventh day (2:1-3), Lamech is distinguished from the generations that have gone before him. He is given by far the greatest space, and uniquely, a speech in which he says, 'If Cain is avenged seven times, then Lamech *seventy-seven* times' (4:24). For good measure, the genealogy of chapter 5, which follows immediately after, also has a character by the name of Lamech, who dies aged 777 (5:31). Enough has been said about these first two genealogies, therefore, to alert us to their interest in the number seven.

That continues in the next genealogy of 5:1-32:

1. Adam
2. Seth
3. Enosh
4. Kenan
5. Mahalalel
6. Jared
7. Enoch
8. Methuselah
9. Lamech
10. Noah

A genealogy of *ten* generations might seem to disappoint our expectations. But we see immediately that the seventh generation, Enoch, is distinguished from all the others. We are told twice that 'Enoch walked with God' (5:22, 24). But even more strikingly, while all of the others receive the death notice, 'and then he died',[48] of Enoch we read, 'then he was no more, because God took him away' (5:24). Once again the seventh generation is distinguished from all of the others.

The remaining genealogies of the primaeval history follow a similar pattern. The Table of Nations takes up most of chapter 10. It lists the nations of the ancient world descended from the sons of Noah, but includes the one exception of Nimrod, the single individual among the nations. If he is omitted, the table contains *seventy* nations. (For more detail, see comments on chapter 10.) The final genealogy is 11:10-26. Like the genealogy of chapter 5 it is composed of ten elements, and just like the final patriarch Noah in that list, so here Terah also has three sons. Placing Eber, the one after whom the Hebrews were named, in fourth position in 11:14-17, makes him the fourteenth since creation, and the seventh generation after Enoch.[49] The genealogy concludes its listing, and with it the primaeval history, with a note concerning the age at which Terah fathered his sons – *seventy* (11:26). So, all the genealogies in chapters 1-11 emphasise, in some way or other, the seventh generation, or place the number seven or a multiple in a prominent position.

This pattern is not found in all biblical genealogies, but a few more examples will demonstrate that we are not making a special case just for the primaeval history. When Joseph's family moves from Canaan to join him in Egypt, a complete listing of the family is given in Genesis 46:8-27. The sons of Jacob are listed, plus the number of sons that each of them had, as follows:

	Son	*Number of Sons*
1.	Reuben	4
2.	Simeon	6
3.	Levi	3
4.	Judah	5
5.	Issachar	4
6.	Zebulun	3
7.	Gad	7
8.	Asher	4
9.	Joseph	2
10.	Benjamin	10
11.	Dan	1
12.	Naphtali	4

Gad is the *seventh* son, and he has *seven* sons. Not only that, but letters of the Hebrew alphabet were used as numerals, just as Roman letters were. The numerical value of Gad's name is *seven*. The letter 'g' = 3 and 'd' = 4. There were no vowels in the Hebrew alphabet, so 'a' has no value.

Just in case we miss the significance of these figures, the text tells us explicitly, 'All those who went to Egypt with Jacob – those who were his direct descendants, not counting his sons' wives – numbered sixty-six persons. With the two sons who had been born to Joseph in Egypt, the members of Jacob's family, which went to Egypt, were *seventy* in all' (Gen 46:26-27). So, this list has a *seventh* son having *seven* sons whose name is worth *seven*, in a family totalling *seventy*, just as there were *seventy* nations in the table of chapter ten. One suspects that a list with these characteristics is providing more than simply bald genealogical data.

The preoccupation with the number seven in genealogies is not limited to the book of Genesis, nor even to the Old Testament. The New Testament commences with the genealogy of Christ, tracing his ancestry back to Abraham, the father of Israel (Matthew 1:1-17). Matthew divides this family tree into three sections, and then explicitly provides the number of generations in each section (1:17):

1. Abraham to David   14 generations
2. David to the Babylonian exile   14 generations
3. Babylonian exile to Christ   14 generations

Each section has the same number of generations, which is a multiple of seven. Matthew's reason for presenting Christ's genealogy this way is probably because he wants to present him as the Messiah. The main messianic title for Christ used by Matthew throughout his gospel and which he puts at the head of this genealogy, is 'Son of David' (Matt. 1:1). And the numerical value of 'David' is fourteen.

Luke also gives a genealogy for Christ, but he traces his ancestry back not merely to Abraham, but all the way to Adam (Luke 3:23-38). If you take the time to count the generations, you will find that there are *seventy-seven*.

Let me repeat, by no means do all of the biblical genealogies show these repeated patterns. But all the genealogies in Genesis 1-11 do. What is the significance of that?

Throughout history some people have been fascinated by the use of numbers or other repeated patterns found in Scripture, and have used these as the basis for bizarre predictions about world history.[50] That is not my intention here. What we have seen in some biblical genealogies is not a code that can be cracked by those who possess secret knowledge. It is much more sober than that. Yet important all the same.

To see the significance of the genealogies in Genesis we need to look at the broad sweep of the book. It contains two main types of literature. On the one hand genealogies, and on the other narratives – that is, the stories that make up the bulk of the book. This alternation between genealogies and narratives is how Genesis divides itself up into sections. The genealogies, as we have seen, are to a degree schematic and predictable. We cannot predict everything about a genealogy before we have read it, but in Genesis 1-11 we very soon learn that the number seven will be prominent. And it is that very predictability that is the main point.

The repeated schematic patterns and design of the genealogies indicate that God is in control of human history. The broad sweep of history and the successive generations are understandable and to a degree predictable. We can see a guiding hand directing history in a certain direction, rather than a mere random collection of events. When God created the heavens and the earth he demonstrated his sovereignty, and the Genesis account of creation underlines that. God created in six days, rested on the seventh day, blessed and sanctified it, and that amounts to 'a genealogy of the heavens and the earth' (2:4). The pattern established in that introductory genealogy of creation, where the seventh element is the most significant, is then adopted in the human genealogies that follow. As God showed his sovereignty over creation, he demonstrates it in human history.

If we now turn to the narratives, we find something very different. The stories are not predictable or schematic. How a story will develop is quite open-ended. For example, the Man and Woman were not compelled to eat fruit from the forbidden tree, nor did Cain have to kill his brother. And the reasons why characters act as they do is often not explicitly given. For example, why did the Serpent tempt the Woman, Cain kill his brother, Lamech slay his opponent, etc? We simply cannot say just by looking at the story. One reason why the stories are written this way is to emphasise that their characters have free will. The end of the story is not determined from the outset, but depends on the free motives of its characters – sometimes revealed and sometimes not. This becomes increasingly clear as the book progresses and its individual stories become more detailed. For example, we see Abraham believing God's amazing promise that he will father a son (15:6), but then questioning God's plan for providing that same child (17:17, 18). When he thinks God will destroy Sodom, he tries to persuade God to change his mind (18:22-32), yet when God tells him to sacrifice his own son, he accepts without any argument (22:1, 2). This inconsistency makes it difficult to predict what Abraham will do next. He is a typical human being with conflicting motives, who exercises his freedom to respond to God in more than one way. And this is typical of the narratives in Genesis. They indicate, in contrast to the genealogies, that not everything in life is predictable or understandable. Life contains mystery and ambiguity and the uncertainty of not knowing how we ourselves, let alone others, will react in a situation.

So, genealogies and narratives are quite different and seem to make conflicting points. *The genealogies*: life is under the guidance of God and is predictable and understandable. *The narratives*: life is open-ended and how it works out depends on all kinds of factors. These apparent contradictions actually make a significant point about God's ways in the world. A conundrum that has puzzled the faithful over the centuries is the relationship between God's sovereignty and human free will. Both divine sovereignty (e.g. Exod. 9.12; Rom. 8:29, 30) and human free-will (e.g. Josh. 24:15; John 7:17) are affirmed in Scripture. But how can both be true? For if God is absolutely sovereign, then we are not free. And if we are absolutely free, then God is not sovereign. The Bible does not provide a solution to this problem. Rather, it presents the issue as a paradox, that is, the contradiction is only apparent, not real. If we wish to see examples of how we are free to choose our own destiny, then we can read the narratives and see Adam, Eve, Cain, Lamech, Abraham and the rest do just that. But if all we had was human free will, we would be in a real dilemma. The genealogies of Genesis 1-11 remind us of the other side of the equation. Through their repetitions and predictability they witness to God's leading in human history. They show that life is not merely a random collection of events driven by human free will. There is meaning to life. In other words: God is sovereign. So, even the 'tedious' genealogies are profound statements that help us to live in God's world.

Some individual elements in chapter 5 are worth noting. First, there are some interesting comparisons with the family tree in 4:17-24. Each of these genealogies traces the line of descent through one person in each generation, but in the final generation, three sons are mentioned, Jabal, Jubal and Tubal-Cain, sons of Lamech (4:20-22), and Shem, Ham and Japheth, sons of Noah (5:32). Each contains different characters with the same name: Enoch (4:17-18; 5:19-24) and Lamech (4:18-24; 5:25-31). Others have very similar names: Cain (4:17) and Kenan (5:9-14); Irad (4:18) and Jared (5:15-20); Mehujael (4:18) and Mahalalel (5:12-17); Methushael (4:18) and Methuselah (5:21-27).

The many parallels in these two separate lines of descent suggest that human history is developing along similar lines. But one major difference indicates that they are heading towards a different conclusion.

Only one speech is recorded in each genealogy, each time by a character called Lamech.

The first Lamech boasts about how he murdered a man for merely wounding him (4:23). The second Lamech, using a play on words, names his son *Noah*, saying 'He will comfort (*nāham*) us in the labour and painful toil of our hands caused by the ground the Lord has cursed' (5:29). We are not told why Lamech had such a positive view of his son. But when we look back on this after reading the story of the Flood, it is striking that the line of Cain concludes with one who took life, while the line of Seth concludes with one who saved life.

Even in the line of Seth, however, all is not well. First, at the beginning we are reminded that God created Adam in his image (5:1). When Adam fathered Seth, he was in the image and likeness of *Adam* (5:3). The relationship between God and human beings is diluting as the generations move on. Second, before chapter 5, only two deaths had been recorded, and both of those people had been murdered (4:8, 23). But this genealogy provides a cascade of death notices none, as far as we know, caused by murder. With one exception every generation concludes with the stark statement 'and then he died'. The exception is Enoch, who 'walked with God' and 'then he was no more, because God took him away' (5:24). But even walking with God does not guarantee avoiding death, for Noah did the same (6:9), and even he died (9:29). All humanity lives under the shadow of death. But matters are about to get much worse.

---

[45] The following chart is based on that by Wenham, Genesis 1-15, p. 131.

[46] The NIV consistently translates the word inaccurately and misleadingly as 'account'.

[47] Some people see this statement as the first line of the following account. However, with many others, I am convinced that 2:4a is rather the conclusion of the preceding account. The features of the text I will highlight seem to establish this.

[48] We have to wait until 9:29 for Noah's notice.

[49] J.M. Sasson, 'A Genealogical "convention" in Biblical Chronography?' *Zeitschrift für die alttestamentliche Wissenschaft 90* (1978), pp. 171-85 (176).

[50] For a recent example see M. Drosnin, *The Bible Code* (London: Weidenfield and Nicolson, 1997).

CHAPTER SEVEN
From Order to Chaos & Back Again
Genesis 6

The story of the Flood takes up most of chapters 6-9. This long account is actually a huge insertion into Noah's genealogical note. This can be seen clearly if we look at the way in which the genealogy of chapter 5 is put together. With only minor additions, each generation is described as follows:

1. When A had lived x years
2. he became the father of B.
3. and after he became the father of B, A lived y years.
4. and had other sons and daughters.
5. Altogether, A lived z years
6. and then he died.

Noah's entry begins in similar fashion (5:32):
1. After Noah was 500 years old
2. he became the father of Shem, Ham and Japheth.
   Naming three sons rather than one suggests that Noah's will be the final entry in the list (as with the threefold entries in 4:20-22 and 11:26). But then Noah's genealogy breaks off prematurely, and chapter 6 begins the background to the story of the Flood. It is only when we have read the whole of that story that the remaining elements of Noah's genealogy are provided in 9:28-29, modified to take account of the intervening Flood:
3. After the flood Noah lived 350 years.
4. ─────────────────────────────────
5. Altogether, Noah lived 950 years,
6. and then he died.

By inserting the Flood story as a large parenthesis into Noah's genealogy, there can be no doubt about who is the main character of that story. But even this great hero eventually dies, like all those who perished in the Flood.

The opening words of the introduction to the Flood account (6:1-4), are the most difficult and obscure in the whole book. The problem centres on the information that, 'the sons of God saw that the daughters of men were beautiful, and they married any of them they chose' (6:2).

Who are 'the sons of God' and the 'daughters of men'?[51]

There are two main suggestions:

First, that the 'sons of God' are the righteous descendants of Seth and the 'daughters of men' are the wicked descendants of Cain. It is true that 6:1-4 is preceded by the genealogies of these two people (4:17-24; 5:1-32). However, the text does not make any explicit connection. In the genealogy of 4:17-24, Cain and Lamech are certainly wicked, but we are told nothing about the rest. The genealogy of 5:1-32 highlights the righteousness of Enoch, and we are later told the same about Noah (6:9). But what about the rest? We know nothing. Also, these marriages took place 'when men (*hā'ādām*) began to increase in number on the earth and daughters were born to them' (6:1). The term 'men' (*hā'ādām*) in this verse must mean humanity in general. The next verse refers to 'the daughters of men (*hā'ādām*)'. If these women are specifically daughters of wicked men rather than just women in general, the word for 'men' (*hā'ādām*) must have a different meaning here than it did in the previous verse. But the text gives no clue that it should.

The second main suggestion for identifying these characters starts by looking at how the term 'sons of god' is used elsewhere in the Bible. For example, 'One day when the sons of God came to attend on Yahweh . . .' (Job 1:6, New Jerusalem Bible). These are clearly non-human characters, and the Hebrew term used is identical with the one in Gen. 6:2. Other versions render them as 'the heavenly beings' (New Revised Standard Version) or 'the divine beings' (Jewish Publication Society Tanakh). So, it is argued, Gen. 6:1, 2 describe how angels cohabited with human women.[52] Such a gross transgression of heavenly order invoked God's anger and resulted in the Flood.

What are we to make of these arguments? The suggestion that angels intermarried with women, when read in the context of the rest of Scripture, seems bizarre, and many will dismiss this possibility on those grounds alone. On the other hand, identifying the sons of God as Sethites and the daughters of men as Cainites, is not without difficulties either for reasons we have already seen. If we confine ourselves to the biblical text alone, it is not clear who they are.

Regardless of their identity, what can we learn from these verses? The passage subtly indicates that the actions of the sons of God will result in disaster by echoing the fateful episode in the garden of Eden. The parallels are clear in Hebrew, though often masked in English translation.

Genesis 3:6
a) 'When the woman saw (r'h)
b) that the fruit of the tree was good (tôb)
c) . . . she took (lqh)'

Genesis 6:2
a) 'the sons of God saw (r'h)
b) that the daughters of men were beautiful (tôb)
c) and they married (lqh)'

Also, both incidents involve couples. And just as God's judgement followed swiftly in the garden, so it does here (6:3), and in the same way limits the human lifespan (3:22-23). These connections tell us something about being human. Although we are now outside the garden, the same principles apply. Banishment from Eden has not changed human behaviour. There is the same impulsiveness and inability to resist temptation. And God does not take that lightly. Just how seriously he takes it soon becomes very clear.

God's assessment of the situation makes very sad reading: 'The Lord saw how great man's wickedness on the earth had become, and that every inclination of the thoughts of his heart was only evil all the time' (6:5). What the Lord saw here contrasts with what God saw in the beginning: 'God saw all that he had made, and it was very good' (1:31). The contrast between universal goodness and universal evil not only passes comment on the path humanity has taken, but also reminds us that the original temptation was 'to know good and evil'. And this is the result. The moral chaos of the world is emphasised all the more by the fact that up to this point in Genesis, everything that has been 'seen' has been 'good' (*tôb*). God sees that his creation is 'good'; the Woman sees that the fruit is 'good' (3:6); the sons of God see that the daughters of men are 'good' (often translated 'beautiful', 6:2).

But now there is no good, only evil. The world started in physical chaos, which God transformed to physical order. The moral and spiritual world has now degenerated from its original ideal order to absolute chaos. As a consequence, we should not be surprised that God's solution is to move the physical world back to its original chaotic state (see below). 'God uses the waters of chaos to eliminate social chaos'.[53]

The most striking aspect of this shocking news is God's emotional involvement. He is not like some impersonal heavenly computer programmed to dole out just rewards and punishments. Genesis shows this through one more of its graphic contrasts. On the one hand God, 'saw how great man's wickedness on the earth had become, and that every inclination of the thoughts of *his heart* was only evil all the time' (6:5). On the other hand, 'The Lord was grieved that he had made man on the earth, and *his heart* was filled with pain' (6:6). So, evil in the human heart produces pain in God's heart. This is a profound insight into God's involvement with us. To understand how profound it is we need to look back to the sin in Eden. Back then God said to the Woman, 'I will greatly increase your pains (*'issābôn*) in childbearing; with pain (*'eseb*) you will give birth to children' (3:16). To the Man he said, 'Cursed is the ground because of you; through painful toil (*'issābôn*) you will eat of it all the days of your life' (3:17). Now we learn that God's 'heart was filled with pain (*'āsab*)' (6:6). The words used to describe the Woman's pain in childbirth, the Man's painful work, and the pain in God's heart, are all derived from the same Hebrew root (*'sb*). In other words, just as people experience the pain of sin in their life, so God experiences the pain of human sin. God shares in our experience and suffers because of our sin.[54] As we follow the biblical story onwards it will eventually arrive at Calvary, where the incarnate son of God took that painful participation to its ultimate end.

Many people have difficulty with this biblical picture of God, because it seems to make him too human. However, the language we use when we talk of God often employs abstract philosophical terms. So God, we say, is eternal, omnipresent, omniscient, immutable, etc. But that is not the language of the Bible itself. What the Bible emphasises about God is not his abstract attributes, but his actions and feelings. God thinks, speaks, pities, loves, is angry, and so on (e.g. Exodus 34:6). Now, all language we use about God is human language, the philosophical no less than the emotional. But the Bible does make it absolutely clear that God is a being who can be experienced personally. It is not possible to have a personal relationship with the God who is defined in abstract philosophical terms. To experience him we need the God of the Bible. So, we should not be surprised when the introduction to the Flood story emphasises the emotional involvement of God with his creation. What he is about to do is not taken lightly, for God himself suffers in this dilemma.

Comparing the biblical flood account with other ancient flood accounts enriches our understanding, just as when we compared the Genesis creation account with others from the ancient near east. On the one hand, there are similarities between Genesis and other flood stories. For example, common elements include the gods deciding to destroy the world and a hero who builds a boat surviving the catastrophe.

But these stories form a marked contrast with the Genesis story on more significant issues. The motivation for the flood in the Mesopotamian Atrahasis epic is that humanity is making so much noise that the god Enlil finds it difficult to sleep. It is not entirely clear what the noise actually is. Suggestions include human overpopulation or the din of injustice. But questions of morality or justice are certainly not obvious in the epic. What is more, the actions of Enlil in sending the flood as a solution to the problem are criticised within the epic as lacking justification, which suggests strongly that the flood was not sent in response to human violence or immorality. The account in Genesis forms a big contrast, by showing God's moral justification for punishment yet at the same time his emotional involvement with his creatures.

Unlike the gods of Israel's neighbours, therefore, the God of Genesis is not capricious.[55] The salvation of the hero in the Mesopotamian accounts also differs radically. The gods decide to destroy all humanity, but the god Enki (or Ea), divulges this information to the hero, advising him to build a boat to escape the flood and thus thwart the wish of the assembly of the gods. This picture of conflict among the gods is commonplace in the literature of Israel's neighbours, but totally lacking in the Bible's depiction of the one God who enacts his own will. So similar stories present radically different views of how God relates to us.

Before we look at some of its details, let us take in the broader view of the structure of the Flood account. We have already seen an example of 'chiasm' in 2:4, where the second part of a sentence or short passage echoes the first part, but in reverse order. Another example is found in 4:4-5:

A The Lord looked with favour
B on Abel and his offering,
B but on Cain and his offering
A he did not look with favour.

Such arrangements are common, and often do not hold any significance for interpretation. The Hebrews, and other ancient peoples, apparently appreciated the rhythms of such constructions. When we remember that the majority of ancient peoples would have heard these texts being read out aloud, rather than reading the words on the page themselves, we shall see that these patterns would enable them to remember what they had heard. In just the same way, for example, a poem that employs rhyme is easier to memorise than a block of plain prose. However, there are occasions where a chiasm becomes much more elaborate (technically called a palistrophe), and

here the arrangement often seems to give insight into the
meaning of the passage. The Flood story is one of those
places. Notice how, in the following diagram, the second half of
the story is the mirror image of the first.

A Noah and his three sons (6:9-10)
  B Violence in God's creation (6:11-12)
    C God's first speech: resolution to destroy (6:13-22)
      D God's second speech: command to enter the ark (7:1-10)
        E Beginning of the flood (7:11-16)
          F The rising flood waters (7:17-24)
            G GOD REMEMBERS NOAH (8:1a)
          F* The receding flood waters (8:1b-5)
        E* The drying of the earth (8:6-14)
      D* God's third speech: command to leave the ark (8:15-19)
    C* God's resolution to preserve order (8:20-22)
  B* God's fourth speech: covenant blessing and peace (9:1-17)
A* Noah and his three sons (9:18-19)[56]

Each section in this structure complements its matching block
of text. For example, the whole account is bracketed by Noah
and his three sons (A/A*). The violence with which the account
starts contrasts with God's covenant of blessing and peace with
which it concludes (B/B*). One can then compare all the
matching sections until one comes to the central statement in
8:1a, which marks the turning point of the whole account. 'But
God remembered Noah and all the wild animals and the
livestock that were with him in the ark'. Surely God had not
forgotten Noah and then suddenly remembered the plight he
was in. Of course not. For example, both Rachel and Hannah
are unable to have children, but God 'remembers' them, with
the result that they both become pregnant (Genesis 30:22, 23;
1 Samuel 1:19, 20). When the Israelites were being oppressed
as slaves in Egypt, 'God heard their groaning and *he
remembered* his covenant with Abraham, with Isaac and with
Jacob' (Exodus 2:24).

When God 'remembers' people he acts on their behalf; he
saves them from their dilemma. So, right in the centre of the

Flood story we have an act of salvation.

On the other hand, the story of the Flood is clearly a story of judgement on human wickedness. So one thing this story tells us is that *the God who judges is the same God who saves*. We need to avoid two extremes in how we view God, because either of them can twist our relationship with him. If God is only a God of judgement, then we will live in constant fear. For, as Calvin said, if humanity 'were to be dealt with according to their deserts, there would be a necessity for a daily deluge.'[57] On the other hand, if God is only a God of forgiveness and salvation, then we will not see how much our sin pains God. The Flood story shows us how these two aspects should be kept in balance.

Another significant point also emerges from the structure of the story. In the creation account God brought order out of chaos. The first half of the Flood story shows the reverse of that. As the earth is inundated with water, it returns to its original watery condition before God said, 'Let there be light!' (1:3). It returns to *tōhû wābōhû*. The second half of the story shows the reverse movement, as God brings the earth back from chaos to order once more. These movements of physical order and chaos mirror the moral world. Humanity has degenerated from the moral order established at the beginning to the moral chaos where, 'every inclination of the thoughts of [the human] heart was only evil all the time' (6:5). In the middle of that physical and moral chaos, 'God remembered Noah', his faithful remnant on earth.

Yet order and chaos are not the only points of contact that the flood has with the creation story. There are many more, and looking at only a selection of these will highlight how important they are for understanding the Flood.

Flood Story 8:1	Creation Story 1:2
'he sent a wind (*rûah*) over the earth, and the waters receded.'	'the Spirit (*rûah*) of God was hovering over the waters.'

The original Hebrew is even closer than most English versions suggest. In both creation and flood the earth is covered by water, a *rûah* is moving over its surface, and dry land eventually appears.

8:17	1:22
'... the birds, the animals, and all the creatures that move along the ground – so they can multiply on the earth and be fruitful and increase in number upon it.'	'God blessed them and said, "Be fruitful and increase in number and fill the water in the seas, and let the birds increase on the earth." '

Just as God blessed the animals with fertility at creation, those that survive the Flood receive the same blessing. God's world will continue to be productive.

8:21	2:7
' "Never again will I curse the ground (*'ᵃdāmâ*) because of man (*'ādām*)" '	'the Lord God formed the man (*'ādām*) from the dust of the ground (*'ᵃdāmâ*)' (see also 3:17)

The play on words between man (*'ādām*) and the ground (*'ᵃdāmâ*) defined his relationship to the earth at creation. It continues to do so after the Flood.

9:1, 7	1:28
'Then God blessed Noah and his sons, saying to them, "Be fruitful and increase in number and fill the earth. . . . As for you, be fruitful and increase in number; multiply on the earth and increase upon it." '	'God blessed them and said to them, "Be fruitful and increase in number; fill the earth. . . ." '

While the blessing of fertility on human beings is repeated after the Flood, there is a significant difference in how they will relate to the animals, as the following comparison shows.

9:2, 3

'The fear and dread of you will fall upon all the beasts of the earth and all the birds of the air, upon every creature that moves along the ground, and upon all the fish of the sea; they are given into your hands. Everything that lives and moves will be food for you.'

1:28

'Rule over the fish of the sea and the birds of the air and over every living creature that moves on the ground.'

Dominion over the animals continues as before, but with this difference. The original command to rule over the animal creation was given when human beings were vegetarians (1:29, 30). So, the human rule was limited. Now that all creatures can be eaten, the world will be a more brutal place.

9:13

' "I have set my rainbow in the clouds, and it will be the sign of the covenant between me and the earth." '

2:3

'And God blessed the seventh day and made it holy, because on it he rested from all the work of creating that he had done.'

At first sight there seems to be little connection between these two verses. But they are probably the most striking of all the parallels between creation and the flood. At the end of the flood God set the rainbow in the sky as the sign of the covenant that he would never again destroy the earth with water. At the end of creation God sanctified the seventh day. It is not stated explicitly at that point, but the Sabbath is also a sign of the covenant. For example, ' "The Israelites are to observe the Sabbath, celebrating it for the generations to come as a lasting covenant. It will be a sign between me and the Israelites for ever" ' (Exodus 31:16). The Old Testament refers to only three items as being the signs of a covenant: the Sabbath, the rainbow and circumcision (see Gen. 17:11). One of them concludes creation (Sabbath), and another concludes the flood (the rainbow). The new worlds that emerged from the waters at creation and the flood are both under the blessing of God. He is as involved in this world as he was with the one that perished beneath the waters.

In all these details we should not lose sight of the story's central character, Noah. The rest of humanity is utterly wicked, but 'Noah was a righteous man, blameless among the people of his time, and he walked with God' (6:9). He is not the first person to be described in this way. Enoch also had 'walked with God' (5:24). That is not their only similarity. The genealogy of chapter 5 repeats its refrain, 'and then he died,' for all the generations before and after Enoch. But not for Enoch himself. He 'was no more, because God took him away' (5:24). He is spared death. In a similar way, Noah, who also walked with God, was spared the universal death sentence that the rest of humanity suffered in the flood.

We are given glimpses of how Noah might have walked with God. For example, in response to God's instructions, 'Noah did everything just as God commanded him' (6:22). This is in marked contrast to the rest of rebellious humanity. In fact, Noah's unquestioning obedience is like that of inanimate matter in the creation account, where God had only to speak and it was done. The quality of his relationship with God is all the more remarkable when we realise the significance of God's speech, ' "Go into the ark, you and your whole family, because I have found you righteous in this generation" ' (7:1). The two uses of 'you' in this sentence are expressed differently in the Hebrew, but both are in the singular. Therefore, many modern translations render the verse as, ' "for I have seen that *you alone* are righteous before me in this generation" ' (NRSV).[58] In other words, Noah not only contrasts with the world in general, but also with his own family. He demonstrates that a relationship with God is possible despite tremendous peer pressure.

Our moral standards are so often decided by the majority opinion. But a common theme found in Scripture is that of the 'righteous remnant'. For example, when the whole crowd bowed down to Nebuchadnezzar's image, the three friends

Shadrach, Meshach and Abednego stood upright (Daniel 3:9-12). The quality of our relationship with God is revealed in a crisis. And Noah's walk with God is revealed as the rest of the world is judged. He is also an illustration of the impact that an individual can have, for good or ill, on the world. The apostle Paul presents both sides of this picture: 'For if, by the trespass of the one man, death reigned through that one man, how much more will those who receive God's abundant provision of grace and of the gift of righteousness reign in life through the one man, Jesus Christ. . . . For just as through the disobedience of the one man the many were made sinners, so also through the obedience of the one man the many will be made righteous' (Romans 5:17-19). The same general principle is at work here in the story of the Flood. Just as the single sin committed in Eden affected all humanity, so the righteousness of Noah alone saves humanity from total annihilation.

A striking fact about Noah in this account is that he is totally silent. Before the Flood, throughout preparations for it, and while the ark floats on the waters, Noah says not a word. The story underlines not what he says, but what he does. He is the obedient servant of God. Even when the ark is grounded on top of the mountain, Noah does nothing until God gives the command. The picture of Noah as unswervingly righteous and obedient forms a strong contrast to the Man and Woman in the garden. This might raise hopes that a totally new beginning awaits humanity once his family disembarks. If that is what we expect, then we are gravely disappointed.

If we learn a lot about Noah in this story, we learn just as much about God. His motivation for sending the Flood is set out clearly at the outset. Wickedness is rampant and the human heart is evil. In this light, God's reason for promising never to send a flood again seems strange at first sight. He says, ' "Never again will I curse the ground because of man, even though every inclination of his heart is evil from childhood. And never again will I destroy all living creatures, as I have done" ' (8:21).

First, it is clear that any hopes we had for a better world after the Flood were misplaced. The human heart will continue to be evil. So, the Flood has changed nothing. It might have destroyed many evil people, but it has not changed human nature. In other words, punishment has not solved the problem of human sin. If we want a solution to sin itself, it will have to be by another means. We already saw how God suffered because of human sin at the Flood (6:5, 6). The New Testament builds on this to show how God took suffering upon himself. Christ suffered and died on our behalf, and by that means provided the solution to human sin. As Christ himself said, ' "The Christ will suffer and rise from the dead on the third day, and repentance and forgiveness of sins will be preached in his name to all nations" ' (Luke 24:46, 47).

Secondly, God's vow not to destroy the earth raises an obvious question. If, in the future, God will not send a flood despite the depravity of humanity, why did he do so in the time of Noah? Clearly something has changed. In 6:5-7 the evil in the human heart caused God to destroy the earth. In 8:21 he once again sees the same evil in the human heart and decides he will never again destroy. In both places the evil human heart causes God to change his mind. On the first occasion, God says, 'I am sorry that I have made them' (6:7, NRSV). In other words, God changes his mind about humanity. On the second occasion, he changes his mind again, not about humanity but about the punishment he will send. The evil in the human heart after the flood shows that people have not changed their attitude to God. But God's decision shows that he has changed his attitude toward humans. From now on, he will show even more grace than he has in the past.

The flood was the judgement that the world actually deserved; the rainbow symbolises the grace that it does not deserve.

The rainbow is not a sign of a new covenant merely between God and human beings. It is far more comprehensive. It will be 'between me and you and all living creatures of every kind' (9:15). At the heart of the flood story 'God remembered Noah' (8:1). Now, forever after the Flood, when God sees the rainbow, he will 'remember the everlasting covenant between God and all living creatures of every kind on the earth' (9:16). This, despite the fact that humanity still remains wicked. The fact that he never will spells out the depth of his grace. Taken as a whole, therefore, the flood story teaches us as much about God's grace as about his judgement. His grace limits his judgement, not vice-versa. 'For it is by grace you have been saved, through faith – and this not from yourselves, it is the gift of God – not by works, so that no-one can boast' (Ephesians 2:8, 9).

The final episode concerning Noah (9:20-29) is often skipped over, either because it is seen as unseemly or just too obscure. However, it repays closer investigation. We've already seen how some Genesis stories are told so as to recall a previous one. For example, the story of Cain and Abel had numerous points of contact with the Garden of Eden. And so does this present passage. Just as the creation account was followed by a sin, so also the story of recreation, the Flood. No sooner has Noah started to work the soil and grow grapes, than an offence clearly echoing the one in chapter 3 occurs.

	Chapter 3	Chapter 9
Role of fruit	the fruit of the knowledge of good and evil (v. 6)	grapes from Noah's vine-yard (v. 20, 21)
Nakedness	they knew that they were naked (v. 7)	Noah lies naked (vv. 21-23)
Curses	Uttered by the offended party – God (vv. 14-19)	Uttered by the offended party – Noah (vv. 25-27)
Covering nakedness	God clothes Man and Woman with animal skins (v. 21)	Shem and Japheth cover Noah with a garment (v. 23)

But what exactly is the offence committed in this passage? The answer to that question has exercised many minds over many years. The passage is not clear – perhaps deliberately so. Nevertheless, we are told that 'Ham, the father of Canaan, saw his father's nakedness and told his two brothers outside' (9:22). While biblical people were extremely modest, Noah's reaction seems to be disproportionate to the offence, if all that Ham did was accidentally see Noah exposed when he was drunk. But note that Noah delivers his curses when he discovers 'what his youngest son *had done to him*' (9:24). This is a strange way to express matters if all his son did was to tell his brothers that he'd seen their father without clothes on. There is a possibility, however, that more than just seeing was involved. Some other texts that refer to 'seeing nakedness (*'erwâ*)' use it to describe having sexual relations with someone. For example, 'If a man marries his sister, the daughter of either his father or his mother, and they have sexual relations (literally, he sees her nakedness and she sees his nakedness) . . .' (Leviticus 20:17). Without expanding on this point, there is at least a possibility that there is more to this incident than meets the eye.

This obscure episode with possible sexual overtones is not the first of its type. We came to similar conclusions when looking at 6:1-4, concerning the sons of God and daughters of men. That episode was even more obscure than this one, and also has possible sexual overtones – with the sons of God entering into possible illicit sexual relations with the daughters of men. Just as strikingly, these two stories bracket the entire Flood account. The first story follows on from the first part of Noah's genealogy, and the second story introduces the second part of his genealogy. If we return to the structure of the account, in the form of a chiasm, we can now expand the number of corresponding passages in the following manner:

Noah's genealogy A (5:32)
　　Sin: Judgement on sinners; 'grace' to Noah (6:1-8)
　　A　Noah and his three sons (6:9-10)
　　　B　Violence in God's creation (6:11-12)
　　　　C　First divine address: resolution to destroy (6:13-22)
　　　　　D　Second divine address: command to enter the ark (7:1-10)
　　　　　　E　Beginning of the flood (7:11-16)
　　　　　　　F　The rising flood waters (7:17-24)
　　　　　　　　G　GOD REMEMBERS NOAH (8:1a)
　　　　　　　F*　The receding flood waters (8:1b-5)
　　　　　　E*　The drying of the earth (8:6-14)
　　　　　D*　Third divine address: command to leave the ark (8:15-19)
　　　　C*　God's resolution to preserve order (8:20-22)
　　　B*　Fourth divine address: covenant blessing and peace (9:1-17)
　　A*　Noah and his three sons (9:18, 19)
　　Sin: Judgement on Canaan; blessing on Shem, Japheth (9:20-27)
Noah's genealogy B (9:28)

When we set out the account in this graphic way, it reiterates what we concluded earlier: the flood does not change human nature. Sin introduces and concludes the Flood story, emerging unscathed from the waters of judgement. The final line of the whole account reminds us that something else has not changed either. The last thing we are told about Noah is, 'and then he died' (9:29). If sin has survived the deluge, then so has death. For as Paul reminds us, 'the wages of sin is death' (Romans 6:23). We will need to keep reading for a little while longer to find hints of how this curse of sin will be overturned.

Out of the numerous insights provided by the flood story, let us reflect briefly on the following:

First, God is emotionally involved in our dilemma. He understands how sin devastates our lives and relationships because he has experienced the pain of sin himself (6:6). The New Testament revelation of Christ's compassionate suffering on our behalf is not an innovation, but a development of this truth.

Second, just as the creation accounts presented God as both almighty and personal, so we learn here that he is both the judge and saviour. God both judges and saves because he cares. He is not apathetic about either our needs or our faults. He is involved in every aspect of our lives. A God who is there.

Third, the sign of the rainbow, symbolising God's unconditional undertaking to sustain life, reveals that the essence of his relationship to the world, and to us, is grace. In the middle of our chaotic lives, God still remembers us.

[51] For a full discussion of all of the problems in these verses, see Wenham, *Genesis 1-15*, pp. 135-47.

[52] This interpretation is found in ancient Jewish writings outside the Old Testament, e.g. 1 Enoch 6:2. Cf Jude 6-7.

[53] J.H. Walton, 'Flood', in T. Desmond Alexander and David W. Baker (eds.), *Dictionary of the Old Testament: Pentateuch* (Downers Grove/Leicester: InterVarsity Press, 2003), p. 323.

[54] See Westermann, *Genesis 1-11*, pp. 410-1.

[55] For a detailed comparison of the biblical and near eastern flood stories, see Walton, 'Flood', pp. 315-26.

[56] For more detail see B.W. Anderson, 'From Analysis to Synthesis: The Interpretation of Genesis 1-11', *Journal of Biblical Literature 97* (1978), pp. 23-39.

[57] J. Calvin (1554), *Genesis* (trans. J. King; Edinburgh: Banner of Truth Trust, 1847), p. 284.

[58] See also e.g., The New American Standard Bible, New Jerusalem Bible, Jewish Publication Society Tanakh.

CHAPTER EIGHT
The Whole World in His Hands

The final remnants of Noah's genealogy that end the flood account are followed immediately by an extensive genealogy of his sons. However, unlike previous family lists which deal with individuals, this one enumerates how from Noah's sons 'the nations spread out over the earth after the flood' (10:32). The story of Babel that follows (11:1-9), tells us how that dispersal started. This is not the only place in Genesis where a summary is provided before the details are spelled out. For example, 1:1 tells us that God created everything, and only then tells us how God did it. If this account were being told chronologically, 11:1-9 would come before chapter 10. But Genesis wants to do more than give a simple chronological account. One of the reasons for putting matters in this order is to highlight connections between the content of chapters 9 and 10. To give just one example, when Noah's family had emerged from the ark God had blessed them, ' "Be fruitful and increase in number and fill the earth" ' (9:1). Chapter 10 shows us in no uncertain terms that they did indeed fill the earth. But we need to wait until the story of Babel (11:1-9), to discover how that came about.

We have already noted how genealogies in chapters 1-11 emphasise the significance of the number seven. (See comments on chapter 5.) We see the same in this table of nations. The list provides six entries in 10:2-7 (Japheth, Gomer, Javan, Ham, Cush and Raamah). The seventh list, however, goes back to Cush and gives an expanded note on his son Nimrod (10:8-12). We learn far more about him and his exploits than about any other character in the list. What is more, we learn that 'the first centres of his kingdom were Babylon . . .' (10:10). Although translated differently here as 'Babylon', the Hebrew word (*bābel*) is exactly the same as 'Babel'. By once again highlighting the seventh element, Nimrod, who founded Babel, the genealogy forges a strong connection with the next episode concerning that same place (11:1-9). The fact that Nimrod's name can be translated as 'We will rebel', makes us anticipate the worst. Not only that, but he is also a 'mighty warrior (*gibbōr*)' (10:8), a term last used to describe the Nephilim who were in the earth when the sons of God cohabited with the daughters of men (6:4). The punishment of the Flood occurred immediately after that. What might we anticipate here?

At first sight this list of nations seems to be exhaustive. But there is an obvious omission – Israel.

We tend to think of the Old Testament as the story of God's people, but the primaeval history gives us many reminders that that is only part of the picture. God is the God of all people. The ark saved humanity.

Noah was not an Israelite, nor was any of the numerous offspring mentioned in this list. The God who created the whole world also punished the whole world. But as the rainbow reminds us, he also shows grace to the whole world. We will soon learn that he plans to expand on that grace (12:1-3).

CHAPTER NINE
Chaos – Again!
Genesis 1:1-2:4a[2]

The first account of the primaeval history began with physical chaos and moved to order and rest on the sanctified seventh day. The last account reverses that move but at a different level. It begins with order and unity with the whole world having 'one language and a common speech' (11:1), but concludes with chaos, not only in confusion of language but in the human rebellion against God's will showing its moral and spiritual chaos. As we shall see later, it is very significant that Genesis 1-11 begins and concludes in a similar way.

The narrative hints right at the start that things might go awry. The human couple were exiled from Eden, which was in the *east* (2:8); the cherubim barred their re-entry 'on the *east* side of the Garden of Eden' (3:24). The murderer Cain was exiled to the land of Nod, '*east* of Eden' (4:16). In this present episode, the Hebrew is unclear whether the people migrated 'eastward' (NIV) or 'from the east' (NRSV). Whichever it is, it makes us anticipate the worst.

The people's ambition is to build a city with a high tower, so that they may make a name for themselves and not be scattered over the whole earth (11:4). This seems straight-forward enough, but what exactly do they wish to do, and why? The building of a city is understandable, but they also want 'a tower that reaches to the heavens'. It is often assumed that they wanted to challenge God – this tower was their attempt to storm the heavens. Or, perhaps, they disbelieved God's promise that he would not send another flood, and the tower was their escape route from the flood waters, should they

come. Both of these might be possible, but neither is stated
explicitly by the Bible. Before the Israelites took the land of
Canaan, the walls of the Canaanite cities were said to be 'up to
the heavens' (Deuteronomy 9:1). This simply means that they
were very tall. So the people of Babel's words might mean no
more than they desired to build a very tall tower – but not
literally to storm God's heaven.

Their first motivation is that they want to make a name for
themselves. Within the Genesis story so far, this is a striking
ambition. So far names have been given by a superior to an
inferior: for example, by God to his creation (1:5, 8, 10); the
Man to the animals (2:20) and, after the curse of male
domination, to his wife (3:20); a mother (4:25, 26) and father
(5:3) to their child. But now, it seems, these people accept no
higher authority and want to make a name for themselves. This
spirit of independence is very similar to the original human sin
back in the garden.

The second reason they give, however, is the more striking.
They do not wish to be scattered throughout the whole world.
But that is God's desire. On two occasions already he has
made it explicit.

At creation human beings were told to 'fill the earth' (1:28).
And God repeated it after the Flood (9:1). But these people
come to the plain of Shinar and decide to settle down in
one place. It is only when we see these points that we can
understand God's punishment. First, the people want to make
a name for themselves, and that is exactly what they get – the
new name of Babel (11:9).

Second, they do not wish to be scattered, but that is what
God engineers by confusing their language: 'From there the
Lord scattered them over the face of the whole earth' (11:9).
The punishment fits the crime. If the main problem was the
building of the city or the tower, then God could merely have
destroyed both of them. Instead, what he did was to change
human existence permanently. Compared to the Flood, therefore, the confusion of human language at Babel is much more
significant. We have seen that the Flood punished sin – but
achieved nothing else. The punishment of Babel still affects us.

In all previous punishments, God's grace had also been shown. After the sin in the garden, death does not follow immediately and God provided clothes for the human couple. Cain is punished, but he is given a mark to protect him. God destroys the sinful world, 'but Noah found favour in the eyes of the Lord' (6:8). The story of Babel, however, has no such example of grace. Our understanding of the primaeval history will not be complete until we discover that element of grace. But that is not until the beginning of the ancestral history in chapter 12.

The primaeval history comes to a rest with another genealogy (11:10-26). To a modern mind this ending seems to be an anticlimax, if not to say dull. But as we have seen, the regularity of the generations, and their schematic and repetitive design, is quite intentional. (See comments on chapter 5.) It provides an appropriate way for this part of Genesis to conclude. God is guiding human history, despite the catastrophes that happen when humans exercise their free will. God is still in control.

CHAPTER TEN
Looking Back; Looking Forward

The aim of this book was to set out on a journey of discovery into the primaeval history of Genesis. It is time now to look back on that journey, and to summarise some of our major findings concerning God and ourselves. We have space here for only a broad sketch of some of the most important aspects and their implications.

To begin with, let's consider five aspects of God revealed in Genesis chapters 1-11.

First, he is a God with universal interests. The opening verse is enough to tell us that: 'In the beginning God created the heavens and the earth.' God is, of course, interested in his chosen nation. But for the moment, that can wait. J. B. Phillips, best known as a translator of the New Testament, wrote a provocative book entitled, *Your God is Too Small*.[59] There is no danger of our having a God who is too small if we accept the message of the primaeval history. For he is not only the God of the universe, but more specifically the God of all human beings. In the beginning he created a Man and a Woman, not a Jew, or a Nigerian, or an Anglo-Saxon. The exhaustive list of nations in chapter 10 summarises his involvement with the whole of humanity. As our modern world increasingly becomes a global village, and as we struggle to live as responsible citizens within it, the primaeval history should be required reading for all people of faith.

Secondly, God is in control. God creates effortlessly, by the sheer authority of his word, as is witnessed by the repeated, 'And God said . . .' of the creation account. This stark contrast to the struggles and battles of many ancient creation myths gives us confidence in the power of God, who has control over matter. It also counters the modern secular article of faith, that all life on earth is the end result of the survival of the fittest, a struggle pure and simple. He not only has control over matter, but he is also the lord of time and space, demonstrated by his creating, naming and separating the basic elements of time and space: day and night; the heavens above; the earth beneath.

If he is lord of time, then history is his arena. He is encountered not only 'back then' but also 'right now'. We can expect to encounter God in our own time and personal experience. If he is the lord of space, then he is never beyond our reach. He is the God who is there – indeed, the God who is here. That is why Genesis stresses that he is the one who rules human destinies, not the astrological influence of the sun, moon and stars.

In fact, perhaps 'rules' is not the best term to use, because in contrast to the fatalism of ancient and modern astrology, God does not want to control us, but gives us *freedom*. (For more on human freedom, see below). Yet at the same time, through his sovereignty, he is guiding human history. Despite sin, he has not cast us adrift. Reflecting on the genealogies we can see, through their repeated patterns and schematic design, the guiding hand of the one who is lord of time and space.

When it seems that our modern world is heading for nuclear suicide, Genesis reassures us that God is guiding the world in his own way and in his own time. And he can afford to do that, of course, because he is eternal. 'In the beginning, God . . . .' He is no Johnny-come-lately on the scene. At his leisure he can take the broad view, fulfilling his purposes unhurriedly, as he sees fit. With a God like that, we might be well advised to be less impatient with the way things are going in this world.

Thirdly, God is not simply the all-powerful transcendent God who reigns over the universe. He is also the intimate and tender God, emotionally involved with his creation. He forms human beings as a potter shapes clay and invests his creative energies in them. We often deal with God as if he were an object for debate, defined by creeds or circumscribed by 'fundamental beliefs'. Even in general conversation we often use philosophical, theological or abstract terms in talking about him. But in the Genesis account God is a character, a personality, not a theological construct. That is to say, he is a God we relate to, with whom we can have a personal relationship. Rather than discussing his attributes, or defining his being, Genesis invites us to know and experience him. After all, we were created in his image. At the very least this means that we were created with a capacity to have a relationship with God. And if that is how he created us, clearly God wants to have a relationship with us. That would not be possible if he were the intellectual God of philosophy or the impassive God of the ancient Greeks. But he isn't. He is a personal God with emotions, who grieves over our sin and suffers with us. We are not alone in our struggles with the injustices of sin in this world. For God understands, feeling and suffering – the results of sin – in his own being. The God who became flesh and suffered on our behalf on the cross is none other than the one whose heart was filled with pain because of human depravity at the time of Noah.

Fourthly, despite the whole dilemma of human sin, he is a God of grace. We do not receive from him what we deserve. Whether we look at, for example, the Man and Woman in the garden with the forbidden fruit in their hand, or Cain standing over his murdered brother, he does not apply the letter of the law. His grace tells us that he is approachable and compassionate. Yet at the same time, he also judges. These are complementary aspects of God's character, not con-tradictory. For example, in the Flood story he both judges and saves. He judges and saves because he cares. He is not apathetic when it comes to dealing with human sin. Apathy as a response to injustice would be the greatest injustice of all. His grace shows that he is compassionate; his judgement shows that there is a limit even to God's patience with injustice. In other words, God does judge, but that is never his first port of call, for his tendency is to apply grace first.

Finally, perhaps the most important of the implications that arise from what God does in these chapters is the importance of spirituality in his scheme. For example, the very fact that it is God who creates the physical world shows that there is more to the world than meets the eye. There is a reality that our physical senses are not capable of comprehending. Therefore, our lives, without this spiritual dimension, are incomplete. We need look no further than the fact that God created us in his image, that is with a capacity to relate to him, to confirm that we were created as spiritual beings. To this we can add God's sanctification of the seventh day of creation. This holy day indicates that time itself has a spiritual dimension. Time is not merely a matter of reckoning years, months, days, hours, minutes and seconds. These form only the framework within which God acts, and is known and experienced.

And as one final example, even the tragedy of Cain and Abel illustrates the significance of the spiritual. We see in this story that only our best is good enough for God. If nothing else, this demonstrates just how important worship is. In recent times many have become rather casual about worship. We tend to look at the practices of former times and judge them as being too formal. Perhaps so. But Genesis reminds us that worship is no nonchalant matter to be done in whatever easygoing manner suits us. The fact that God expects our best shows just how important spirituality is, not simply for us, but more importantly for God himself.

Genesis 1-11 not only reveals something about God, but also about ourselves.

First, we are clearly very significant to God. When creating us he used the climactic plural, 'Let *us*', used of the creation of humans and of nothing else. Also unique is the fact that we were created in the image of God, having the capacity to have a relationship with him. On the one hand this liberates us from the fatalism of the ancients who saw humans merely as slaves to the gods, and also counters modern pessimism that sees no ultimate meaning or purpose in human existence. On the other hand, it points out that with this great privilege comes a responsibility.

As the image of God we are God's representatives on earth, commissioned to represent him correctly in the world. So there are ethical implications that flow from this conviction, not least of which is to be responsible stewards of God's rich and varied world. The privilege of being in his image should produce humility, as should some other aspects of the account. For example, we are not the pinnacle of creation. We might bring God's physical creation to a conclusion, but it is the Sabbath which is its crowning glory. The fact that holy time completes creation points to the holy God, rather than to ourselves, as its centre.

Secondly, we were created as social beings, designed to share our lives with other people in order to be truly fulfilled. When the Man was alone God said, 'It is not good.' Wholesome human relationships are many and varied, and marriage is not the only one. Our modern western society emphasises individualism to such an extent that the social aspect of being human is often devalued. It is no accident that as individualism grows we also see increasing social disintegration. Like Cain, too many seriously question whether they have a responsibility to their 'brother'.

Thirdly, God gave us freedom of choice. We see this illustrated repeatedly in the stories, where the direction taken by the account depends on the decisions made by individuals, such as Eve in the Garden or Cain with his brother. However, with this freedom come responsibilities; our actions have consequences. We were created in the image of God, so we are morally responsible creatures. Too often, however, we value our freedom but do not accept that our actions have repercussions. We flatly disagree (like Cain), or make limp excuses (like the Man and Woman). We crave absolute freedom. But that is not how God created us. The one tree in the garden that was forbidden shows that we operate best as moral beings within boundaries. We achieve our full potential by living in God's world, freely choosing to do so on God's terms. In our sinful world it is those with most power who exercise most freedom, and more often than not oppress those with less power. In Genesis, freedom has nothing to do with power, but a lot to do with accepting the moral boundaries drawn by our creator.

Fourthly, we are sinners. As a consequence, our world is sinful. The path taken by the human story of Genesis 1-11, beginning with the Man and Woman and concluding with Babel, shows that sin affects all that we do and all that we are. Evil defines our lives. Many in our modern world disagree with this. The word 'evil' is still part of our vocabulary, but it is reserved for the most heinous of crimes, and occurs most often in the headlines of tabloid newspapers. But Genesis indicates that the problem is much wider than this. Human relationships have been thrown into radical disarray through sin. This means that most aspects of our society that we take for granted do not conform to God's will. We have exercised our freedom to snub him. Yet despite that, we still live under the blessing of God. The same blessings given at creation (1:28), are repeated with some modification after the flood (9:1-7). So at one and the same time we live under the curse of sin and the blessing of God, just like Cain, who suffers the consequences of murdering his brother, yet at the same time receives God's protective mark of grace. So it is a complex world of good and evil in which we live.

The effect of sin in the world, and how God deals with it, is best understood if we take the time to stand back and trace the significant theme of chaos and order through chapters 1-11. This theme operates at two levels. First, at the physical level, we see it highlighted by the way in which the two major events of the primaeval history are structured. At creation, we started with the earth in a state of disorder (*tōhû wābōhû*). Then, on the first three days of creation God creates environments that are balanced in an ordered way by the next three days, on which God produces creatures to live in or rule over those environments. Finally, God blesses and sanctifies the seventh day, bringing matters to a symmetrical conclusion as Sabbath rest balances the chaos with which the account started. Not only does this demonstrate that God is a God of order, but also that he brings order out of chaos. (See comments on chapter 1 for diagram.) In the same way, the Flood account is structured in a way that highlights movement from physical order to chaos and back to order again. Not only does this once again show

God bringing order out of chaos, but also saving from chaos, as 'God remembered Noah' (8:1; see comments on chapters 6-9 for diagram.)

This theme of chaos/order also operates at the moral/-spiritual level. Initially, there is harmony within creation (1:31), an open relationship between God and human beings (2:15-17), and intimacy between the Man and Woman (2:23-25). This soon disintegrates into disorder, as the human beings blame each other and God (3:12), are in conflict with the natural world (3:15, 17-19), and have their personal relationships characterised by pain and domination (3:16). This moral and spiritual disorder gathers pace. Adam had blamed his wife and God, but Cain murders his brother and claims that he has no responsibility for his welfare (4:8, 9). His exile to 'the land of Nod (wandering)' symbolises the aimless, chaotic state of his relationship with God and his fellow human beings (4:16). If this is not bad enough, it is trumped by Lamech (4:23, 24), and he, in turn, by the whole generation who perished in the flood (6:5).

The intervention of the Flood acts as a punishment for that generation, but cannot prevent moral and spiritual disintegration from continuing. The final narrative of the primaeval history demonstrates that conclusively. Once again people rebel against God's will, and the result is chaos – enshrined in the name of the city, Babel. So the primaeval history concludes with a picture of the nations of the earth in their chaotic rebellion against God. This whole section of Genesis begins and ends with chaos.

Beginning	End
Chapter 1: Physical chaos	Chapter 11: Moral chaos
(tōhû wābōhû)	(Bābel)

The physical chaos with which the earth began was quickly and effortlessly transformed into order by God's command. But the moral chaos with which it ends is far more resistant. How will God return the world to its original moral and spiritual order and harmony? That is the concern of the ancestral history that follows (chapters 12-50).

Looking Forward

The ancestral history is introduced by the genealogy of Terah
(11:27-32), quickly followed by God's call of Abram (12:1-3).
These few verses narrow down the focus from all the nations of
the earth that we met in ch. 10 and the story of Babel, to one
individual family – Abram and his barren wife Sarai.

Chapters 1-11 dealt with universal matters, such as the
creation and destruction of the whole world, the dilemma of all
humanity, cataloguing the nations of the earth, etc. But now we
come to the chosen people in particular.

The beginning of this section of Genesis cannot ignore what
has happened in the previous part. In fact, it would make little
sense without it. At the beginning of the book God's initiative
was to create. Now that his creation has turned against him, his
initiative is to redeem. We have had a hint or two of this before,
of course. For example, in the promise given to the Woman that
her 'seed' would crush the head of the Serpent (3:15). But
some more details of that picture are now filled in.

God's act of creation began with God speaking: 'And God
said, "Let there be light," ' (1:3). His act of redemption also
begins with God speaking: 'The Lord said to Abram, "Leave
your country . . ." ' (12:1). Each of the two major parts of
Genesis begins with a speech from God, because without him
neither creation nor redemption can happen. God spoke his
initial words of creation in the middle of physical chaos. He now
speaks his words of redemption in the shadow of Babel's moral
chaos.

There are numerous significant connections between the end
of the primaeval history and the beginning of the ancestral
history. Two examples will illustrate. The primaeval history ended
with two migrations. The people of the world migrated until they
reached Shinar, where they decided to build their city (11:2-4).
That story concludes with another migration – enforced this
time, as God scatters them over the surface of the earth
(11:8-9).

In a similar way, the ancestral history begins with two
migrations. First, Terah, Abram's father, took his whole family
and 'together they set out from Ur of the Chaldeans to go to

Canaan. But when they came to Haran, they settled there.'
(11:31). Second, Abram is told by God, ' "Leave your country,
your people and your father's household and go to the land
I will show you" ' (12:1). These migrations, however, are set
in very different contexts. The first pair are connected with
judgement at the scattering at Babel; the second pair with
God's new initiative of redemption.

Another striking connection is apparent when we hear the
ambition of the people of Babel. Their motivation for building a
city and tower, they say, is ' "so that we may *make a name* for
ourselves" ' (11:4). When God calls Abram, one of the promises
he gives him is, ' "I will *make your name great*" ' (12:2). What
the people of Babel had attempted to achieve through human
works, God will give to Abram as a gift of his grace.

But why is God showing such an interest in Abram in
particular? Why has he been chosen to be the father of the
chosen nation? And what will this chosen nation achieve?
Indeed, why is it necessary to start from scratch and build up
an entire nation from such small beginnings? Surely there were
plenty of impressive nations already in existence that God
could have adopted. For example, the Egyptians with their
achievements in building, medicine or art; or perhaps one of
several Mesopotamian civilisations and their contributions to
literature and mathematics.

But God did not choose any of them. The familiar doggerel
sums up the point: How odd/of God/to choose/the Jews.[60]
Although sometimes unfortunately used to support anti-semitic
thought, these words sum up the puzzlement of many who read
the story of Abram. For from a human point of view, what did he
and Sarai have to offer God? They were a childless couple of
pensionable age. Yet God chose them as the foundation of his
chosen nation. And that unexpected act of grace is, of course,
just the point. At the debacle of Babel, we noticed that unlike all
other acts of human sin in the primaeval history, there was no
act of God's grace. Not at the time, that is. But here it is now.

God chose the least likely candidates, because he wanted to
establish clearly, once and for all, that what he was going to do
through this chosen nation would be his greatest act of grace.

God's aim is summed up in his final words to Abraham: ' "all peoples on earth will be blessed through you" ' (12:3). Which people could he be talking about? Clearly, all the peoples of the world we have just seen scattered over the surface of the whole world when they rebelled against God at Babel.

Here then is the solution to the human dilemma that was summed up at Babel. God's act of grace is his desire to bless all of humanity rather than to curse it. Ultimately God will bless the whole world through the descendants of Abram.

Genesis never lets us forget that, repeating this promise several times (see 18:18; 22:18; 26:4; 28:14). When God calls Abram he doesn't simply call him to enjoy a special relationship with him. He calls him to be part of God's scheme for history, in which the tragedy we have seen in the primaeval history will finally be overturned, and the world redeemed from the curse of sin. From the chaos of sin God's new order will emerge through the one who came as the descendant of Abraham and the Word of God. 'Since we have been justified through faith, we have peace with God through our Lord Jesus Christ' (Romans 5:1).

---

[59] J.B. Phillips, *Your God is Too Small* (London: Epworth Press, 1956).
[60] Attributed to numerous authors, including Hilaire Belloc, Lord Alfred Douglas, William Norman Ewer, G. K. Chesterton and Ogden Nash.

BIBLIOGRAPHY

Anderson, B., W., `From Analysis to Synthesis: The Interpretation of Genesis 1-11', *Journal of Biblical Literature 97* (1978), pp. 23-39.

Calvin, J. (1554), *Genesis* (trans. J. King; Edinburgh: Banner of Truth Trust, 1847).

Currid, J.D., *Ancient Egypt and the Old Testament* (Grand Rapids: Baker Books, 1997).

Dalley, S., *Myths from Mesopotamia: Creation, the Flood, Gilgamesh, and Others* (Revised; Oxford: Oxford University Press, 2000).

Drosnin, M., *The Bible Code* (London: Weidenfield and Nicolson, 1997).

Hamilton, V.P., *The Book of Genesis: Chapters 1-17* (New International Commentary on the Old Testament; ed. R.K. Harrison; Grand Rapids: Eerdmans, 1990).

Hebrew and Aramaic Lexicon of the Old Testament (HALOT) (ed. L. Koehler and W. Baumgartner; Leiden: Brill Academic Publishers, 2002).

Lucas, E.C., 'Cosmology', in T. Desmond Alexander and David W. Baker (eds.), Dictionary of the Old Testament: Pentateuch (Downers Grove/Leicester: InterVarsity Press, 2003) pp. 130-9.

Mitchell, C., *Creationism Revisited* (Grantham: Autumn House, 1999).

Phillips, J.B., *Your God is Too Small* (London: Epworth Press, 1956).

Sailhamer, J.H., *The Pentateuch as Narrative: A Biblical-Theological Commentary* (Grand Rapids: Zondervan, 1992).

Sasson, J.M., 'A Genealogical "convention" in Biblical

BIBLIOGRAPHY

Chronography?' *Zeitschrift für die alttestamentliche Wissenschaft* 90 (1978), pp. 171-85.

Thompson, R.C., 'The Reports of the Magicians and Astrologers of Nineveh and Babylon', in R.F. Harper (ed.), *Assyrian and Babylonian Literature: Selected Transactions with a Critical Introduction* (New York: Appleton, 1904).

Walton, J.H., 'Creation', in T. Desmond Alexander and David W. Baker (eds.), *Dictionary of the Old Testament: Pentateuch* (Downers Grove/Leicester: InterVarsity Press, 2003) pp. 155-68.

———, 'Flood', in T. Desmond Alexander and David W. Baker (eds.), *Dictionary of the Old Testament: Pentateuch* (Downers Grove/Leicester: InterVarsity Press, 2003) pp. 315-26.

Wenham, G.J., *Genesis 1-15* (Word Biblical Commentary 1; Waco, TX: Word Books, 1987).

———, 'Sanctuary Symbolism in the Garden of Eden Story', in *Proceedings of the World Congress of Jewish Studies 9* (1986) pp. 19-25.

Westermann, C. (1974), *Genesis 1-11: A Commentary* (trans. J.J. Scullion; Minneapolis: Augsburg Publishing House, 1984).

Youngblood, R., *The Genesis Debate: Persistent Questions About Creation and the Flood* (Grand Rapids: Baker Book House, 1990).